THE WORD OF WISDOM

A Formula for Health and Healing

by

Bradley R. Wilde, D.C.

*May The Word of Wisdom
guide you to better health!*

Brad

Notice

The information given here is designed to help you make informed decisions about your health using guidance from the Word of Wisdom. It is not intended as a substitute for any treatment that may have been prescribed by your doctor. If you suspect that you have a medical problem, we urge you to seek competent medical help.

Wilde Natural Health Publishing
801 Robertson
Worland, WY 82401
www.drwilde.com
1-866-379-4533

ISBN-13: 978-1479387007
ISBN-10: 1479387002

Printed in the United States of America

Dedicated to my wonderful wife, Debi, who has always been an inspiration to me and has been my greatest supporter.

CONTENTS

Doctrine and Covenants 89

Revelation given through Joseph Smith the Prophet, at Kirtland, Ohio, 27 February 1833 (see History of the Church, 1:327–29). As a consequence of the early brethren using tobacco in their meetings, the Prophet was led to ponder upon the matter; consequently, he inquired of the Lord concerning it. This revelation, known as the Word of Wisdom, was the result. The first three verses were originally written as an inspired introduction and description by the Prophet.

1–9, The use of wine, strong drinks, tobacco, and hot drinks is proscribed; 10–17, Herbs, fruits, flesh, and grain are ordained for the use of man and of animals; 18–21, Obedience to gospel law, including the Word of Wisdom, brings temporal and spiritual blessings.

1 A Word of Wisdom, for the benefit of the council of high priests, assembled in Kirtland, and the church, and also the saints in Zion—

2 To be sent greeting; not by commandment or constraint, but by revelation and the word of wisdom, showing forth the order and will of God in the temporal salvation of all saints in the last days—

3 Given for a principle with promise, adapted to the capacity of the weak and the weakest of all saints, who are or can be called saints.

4 Behold, verily, thus saith the Lord unto you: In consequence of evils and designs which do and will exist in the hearts of conspiring men in the last days, I have warned you, and forewarn you, by giving unto you this word of wisdom by revelation—

5 That inasmuch as any man drinketh wine or strong drink among you, behold it is not good, neither meet in the sight of your Father, only in assembling yourselves together to offer up your sacraments before him.

6 And, behold, this should be wine, yea, pure wine of the grape of the vine, of your own make.

7 And, again, strong drinks are not for the belly, but for the washing of your bodies.

8 And again, tobacco is not for the body, neither for the belly, and is not good for man, but is an herb for bruises and all sick cattle, to be used with judgment and skill.

9 And again, hot drinks are not for the body or belly.

10 And again, verily I say unto you, all wholesome herbs God hath ordained for the constitution, nature, and use of man—

11 Every herb in the season thereof, and every fruit in the season thereof; all these to be used with prudence and thanksgiving.

12 Yea, flesh also of beasts and of the fowls of the air, I, the Lord, have ordained for the use of man with thanksgiving; nevertheless they are to be used sparingly;

13 And it is pleasing unto me that they should not be used, only in times of winter, or of cold, or famine.

14 All grain is ordained for the use of man and of beasts, to be the staff of life, not only for man but for the beasts of the field, and the fowls of heaven, and all wild animals that run or creep on the earth;

15 And these hath God made for the use of man only in times of famine and excess of hunger.

16 All grain is good for the food of man; as also the fruit of the vine; that which yieldeth fruit, whether in the ground or above the ground—

17 Nevertheless, wheat for man, and corn for the ox, and oats for the horse, and rye for the fowls and for swine, and for all beasts of the field, and barley for all useful animals, and for mild drinks, as also other grain.

18 And all saints who remember to keep and do these sayings, walking in obedience to the commandments, shall receive health in their navel and marrow to their bones;

19 And shall find wisdom and great treasures of knowledge, even hidden treasures;

20 And shall run and not be weary, and shall walk and not faint.

21 And I, the Lord, give unto them a promise, that the destroying angel shall pass by them, as the children of Israel, and not slay them. Amen.

1

THE WORD OF WISDOM FORMULA

An Introduction

Tom had two major concerns about his health. Carpal tunnel syndrome affected his hands and wrists so much that the pain and numbness often kept him from being able to do his taxidermy work. He also had low back pain that had plagued him for 30 years as the result of a skiing accident. The past ten years had been especially bad, and his back would *"go out"* at least weekly. Sometimes he would end up in bed for several days. He had been to numerous medical doctors and chiropractors for relief but was told that he would eventually end up in a wheelchair because of his injury.

Eventually, Tom was able to heal both his carpal tunnel syndrome and his back pain by applying the health principles he learned in the Word of Wisdom. Today he can do his taxidermy, shovel wet snow, or do heavy lifting without any pain in his hands or lower back, and it's all because of the Word of Wisdom. These principles have great power to heal, prevent illness and

1

disease, and promote spiritual and physical well-being. They are powerful because they are revealed truths from Heavenly Father. They can help you improve your health and heal yourself.

I have asked this question of many people, *"What do we need to do to receive the health promises contained in the Word of Wisdom?"* The typical response is, *"We need to stay away from tea, coffee, tobacco, alcohol and illegal drugs."* In fact, close to 100% of respondents will answer with something similar. I will then ask if there is more. *"Is there anything else we need to do to receive those promised blessings?"* The response is usually a little slower in coming. The person might add, *"We need to watch our diet,"* or *"We need to stay away from caffeine,"* or he might make a statement like, *"There needs to be moderation in all things."* Occasionally a person might even say, *"We should eat meat sparingly."*

About 50% of respondents in this informal survey recognize there is something additional about

History of the Word of Wisdom

"When (the brethren) assembled together in this room after breakfast, the first they did was to light their pipes, and, while smoking, talk about the great things of the kingdom, and spit all over the room, and as soon as the pipe was out of their mouths a large chew of tobacco would then be taken. Often when the Prophet [Joseph Smith] entered the room to give the school instructions he would find himself in a cloud of tobacco smoke. This, and the complaints of his wife at having to clean so filthy a floor, made the Prophet think upon the matter, and he inquired of the Lord relating to the conduct of the Elders in using tobacco, and the revelation known as the Word of Wisdom was the result of his inquiry." (Young, 1869)

diet we should follow in order to receive the promised blessings, and they have some idea of what those nutritional recommendations are. The remaining 50% either don't know that the Word of Wisdom talks about nutrition, or if they do know, they don't know what it says.

I will then ask them one last question, *"Is there anything else we need to do to receive the health promises contained in the Word of Wisdom?"* A few individuals hazard a guess, but virtually 0% can come up with the third requirement that allows us to receive the blessings of health promised in the Word of Wisdom.

Most members of the church primarily view keeping the Word of Wisdom as a necessary requirement to be a worthy member in good standing, to advance in the priesthood, or to hold a temple recommend. They see it only secondarily as a means to good health. However, for those wanting to receive the full health benefits offered in the Word of Wisdom, it is imperative to realize there is more required than only abstaining from addictive substances like tea, coffee, tobacco, and alcohol.

THE 3 PRINCIPLES OF SPIRITUAL AND TEMPORAL HEALTH

There are three general principles that the Lord expects us to follow in order to receive the promised health blessings. The principles are found in the first half of verse 18 of Doctrine and Covenants 89, with the blessings following.

18 And all saints who remember to KEEP and DO these sayings, walking in OBEDIENCE to the commandments, shall receive...

If we look carefully at this first half of the verse, we see the three principles we must adhere to:

1. **Remember to KEEP these sayings.**
2. **Remember to DO these sayings.**
3. **Walk in OBEDIENCE to the commandments.**

"Keep" and "do" imply different things. When we talk about *keeping* the Word of Wisdom, we generally think of the things we abstain from. We'll call these the *"don'ts."* When we are asked in a temple recommend interview if we *"keep the Word of Wisdom,"* it is generally understood to mean that we abstain from tea, coffee, tobacco, and alcohol. We *"don't"* use them.

But what does it mean to *"DO these sayings"*? Elder LeGrande Richards taught, *"Much emphasis has been placed— and rightly so—on the don'ts of the Lord's law of health, the Word of Wisdom. Adherence to the prohibitions of this commandment helps one avoid taking harmful substances into his body. However, verses 10 through 16 of this revelation give some positive guidelines for maintaining strong, healthy bodies. Let us look now at some of these **do's**"* (Richards 1950). Elder Richards continues by discussing the important nutritional concepts of the Word of Wisdom, calling them the *"do's."* The do's are of such tremendous importance to our health and well-being that we will discuss them in great detail throughout this book. The Lord gave us this information because He knows what we need to *do* to be healthy. Therefore, there is great wisdom in *doing* what He says.

The third principle required of us, while we *keep the don't*s and *do the do's*, is to *walk in obedience to the commandments.* Elder Ezra T. Benson, who was ordained the twentieth apostle early in this dispensation in 1846, gave some excellent insight on what the Word of Wisdom meant to him and to many of the early members at the beginning of the Church.

"When we first heard the revelation upon the Word of Wisdom many of us thought it consisted merely in our drinking tea and coffee, but it is not only using tea and coffee and our tobacco and whiskey, but it is every other evil which is calculated to contaminate this people. The Word of Wisdom implies to cease from adultery, to cease from all manner of excesses, and from all kinds of wickedness and abomination that are common amongst this generation—it is, strictly speaking, keeping the commandments of God, and living by every word that proceedeth from His mouth.

*"This is the way that I understand the Word of Wisdom, consequently we have to keep **all** the commandments, if I understand the matter correctly, in connection with this Word of Wisdom, in order to obtain the blessings, for unless we do keep the commandments of God, and not offend in any one point, we*

have not a full claim upon the blessings promised in connection with this portion of the word of the Lord" (Benson, Ezra T. 1855). From what this early apostle said, it is apparent that walking in obedience to the commandments is an important requirement for receiving *all* the blessings promised us, both temporally and spiritually.

In more recent times, this was attested to by President N. Eldon Tanner. He said, *"You will note that the Lord says 'walking in obedience to the commandments,' which would include* **all** *the commandments"* (Tanner 1972, emphasis retained from original). Just abstaining from coffee, tea, tobacco, and alcohol isn't enough to be fully living the Word of Wisdom. There is so much more to it. Amazing improvements in health and well-being occur when we implement all of the principles taught in the Word of Wisdom. The Word of Wisdom is not just about what we don't use or consume. It is also about what we do consume and how we use its principles to deal with situations and emotions. It's an all-encompassing principle

Sleep and Exercise

There are two principles to good health that are not mentioned in the Word of Wisdom – adequate sleep and physical exercise. Although exercise is not mentioned in the scriptures, the importance of sleep is stated in another revelation. *"...cease to sleep longer than is needful; retire to thy bed early, that ye may not be weary; arise early, that your bodies and your minds may be invigorated"* (D&C 88:124). Church leaders have also commented on their importance.

President Thomas S. Monson taught, *"Nutritious meals, regular exercise, and appropriate sleep are necessary for a strong body"* (Monson 2008).

Elder Richard G. Scott declared their importance to good spiritual health, *"...spiritual communication can be enhanced by good health practices. Exercise, reasonable amounts of sleep, and good eating habits increase our capacity to receive and understand revelation"* (Scott 2012).

with promises of physical, mental, emotional, and spiritual health.

THE 3 PRINCIPLES IN REAL LIFE

So how does this apply to us in real life? Let's return to Tom who had carpal tunnel syndrome and chronic low back pain and see how he applied these three principles of the Word of Wisdom to overcome his symptoms.

Tom was a coffee drinker. He cut way back on his coffee and at the same time increased his consumption of fruits and vegetables and other healthy foods as indicated in the do's of the Word of Wisdom. Within a month his hands were back to normal. Sometimes he had flare-ups of his carpal tunnel symptoms and realized that coffee was still the major cause of those flare-ups. He continued to cut back on coffee until his flare-ups ended completely. Although he wasn't perfect at *keeping the don'ts* and *doing the do's*, he learned to follow those principles closely enough that his carpal tunnel syndrome became a thing of the past.

Tom's low back was a different story. His symptoms did not change despite a change in diet. His back kept going out, and he had frequent episodes severe enough to keep him in bed for days at a time. Most of these episodes he related to lifting something too heavy or straining too hard. One day he was sitting at the kitchen table with his siblings discussing their elderly mother's deteriorating health. Tom felt she should be put in an assisted living facility where some of her needs could be more easily met. She had the necessary money in a savings account, and he felt it was a good way for her to spend it. A couple of Tom's siblings disagreed and felt she would be better off staying at home.

The discussion became heated, and Tom started to get mad. He could see that his siblings were more concerned about their mother spending "their" inheritance than they were about what was best for her. As the conversation progressed, Tom could feel his back getting tighter and tighter. The tension in the room increased, tempers began to flare, and Tom's back tightened even more. Suddenly, he felt a stabbing pain in his back shooting down his leg. His back had gone out even though he had not been doing anything physically strenuous. He was only sitting at the kitchen table.

Tom realized at that moment that it was not what he was doing physically that caused his back to go out; it was what he was thinking and feeling and the stress of the situation. As he reflected on other times his back had gone out, it all began to make sense to him. He could see how emotional stress was a major cause of the instability and chronic pain in his lower back.

Tom decided he needed to work on how he responded to life and learn how to *not* react with anger, or fear, or worry, or guilt. In terms of the third principle of the Word of Wisdom, he needed to *walk in obedience to the commandments* by being more tolerant, compassionate, kind, patient, and forgiving. He needed to have more faith in God and be less judgmental of others. It was not an easy journey because he had to change long-established responses to life situations. He needed to forgive and let go of things. The good news is he was able to do it and it worked. It has been many months since he has had any pain at all in his back.

These three principles of the Word of Wisdom are powerful because they work! In 21 short verses Joseph Smith gives us the most inspiring and enlightening document ever written on how to have good spiritual and temporal health. It is powerful because it is revealed truth from Heavenly Father and not just the opinion of men. His wisdom far surpasses our own. He knew way back in 1833 that we would need this wisdom to deal with the challenges of our times and the great blessings it would bring into our lives.

THE PROMISED BLESSINGS

What are the promised blessings available in this remarkable revelation? They are found in verses 18-21.

18 ... shall receive health in their navel and marrow to their bones.
19 And shall find wisdom and great treasures of knowledge, even hidden treasures.
20 And shall run and not be weary, and shall walk and not faint.

7

21 And I, the Lord, give unto them a promise, that the destroying angel shall pass by them, as the children of Israel, and not slay them. Amen.

Some of these blessings are temporal and some are spiritual. The heading to section 89 says, *"Obedience to gospel law, including the Word of Wisdom, brings **temporal and spiritual blessings**."*

President Ezra Taft Benson expounded on these two types of blessings, emphasizing the greater importance of the spiritual ones,

"The temporal promise for obedience is: 'They shall receive health in their navel and marrow to their bones; ... [they] shall run and not be weary, and shall walk and not faint.' (D&C 89:18.20)

*"I have always felt, however, that the greater blessing of obedience to the Word of Wisdom and all other commandments is spiritual. Listen to the spiritual promise: 'All saints who remember to keep and do these sayings, walking in obedience **to the commandments** ... shall find wisdom and great treasures of knowledge, even hidden treasures.' (D&C 89:18-19.)*

*"Some have thought this promise was contingent on just keeping the provisions of the Word of Wisdom. But you will notice we must walk in obedience to **all** the commandments. Then we shall receive specific spiritual promises. This means we must obey the law of tithing, keep the Sabbath day holy, keep morally clean and chaste, and obey all other commandments. When we do all this, the promise is: They 'shall find wisdom and great treasures of knowledge, even hidden treasures'" (D&C 89:19)* (Benson, Ezra Taft 1983, emphasis retained from the original).

The final promise, *"... that the destroying angel shall pass by them... and not slay them..."* (D&C 89:21), is also both a temporal and spiritual promise. Elder Rudger Clawson commented on the temporal part of this blessing. He said that the Lord *"...will bless (his people) and he will preserve them and carry them along until they shall have fulfilled the measure of their creation and accomplished their work, if they will observe to keep and do these sayings and render obedience to his law"* (Clawson 1920). In other words, by obeying the Word of

Wisdom, we will not experience a physical death before our time.

President Boyd K. Packer pointed out the spiritual aspect of this promise. *"... if we walk in obedience to these commandments... there is spiritual death which you need not suffer. If you are obedient, that spiritual death will pass over you, for 'Christ our passover is sacrificed for us,' the revelation teaches (1 Cor. 5:7)"* (Packer 1996).

The temporal and spiritual blessings we receive by obeying all the principles of the Word of Wisdom are remarkable! Better physical health, greater wisdom and knowledge, and the destroying angel to pass us by are promised blessings worth striving for.

THE WORD OF WISDOM FORMULA

The Word of Wisdom is a simple, yet profound formula that blesses us with a clear and precise understanding of how to obtain temporal and spiritual health and well-being. Receiving all the promises possible is contingent upon obeying all three principles of *keeping the don'ts, doing the do's* and o*beying the commandments*. Our willingness and ability to keep these principles, as well as the blessings we receive, *vary* according to our understanding, desires, and faith. How we apply these three principles in our lives determines the blessings we receive. The principles and promises of the Word of Wisdom are *variables* just like in a mathematical formula.

In mathematics or science a formula is a rule or statement written in algebraic symbols. For example, the formula to calculate the perimeter of a rectangle is: $(2 \times L) + (2 \times W) = P$. Here, L = length, W = width and P = perimeter. These three letters are all *variables* and change with the size of the rectangle being measured. So if $L=5$ and $W=3$, then $P=16$. If the length and width are larger numbers, then the perimeter of the rectangle will be larger too.

The Word of Wisdom Formula for receiving promised blessings looks like this:

THE WORD OF WISDOM FORMULA

KEEP THE DON'TS	+	DO THE DO'S	+	OBEDIENCE TO COMMANDMENTS	=	PROMISED BLESSINGS

OR

VARIABLE K + VARIABLE D + VARIABLE O = VARIABLE P

Here, *K = keeping the don'ts, D = doing the do's, O = obedience to the commandments,* and *P = promised blessings.* The degree of blessings we receive on the right side of the formula varies according to our degree of understanding and compliance with the variables on the left. The good news is that many members of the Church receive the promised blessings of the Word of Wisdom with or without even knowing its qualifications. They abstain from harmful substances, eat well and keep the commandments, so the Lord blesses them automatically.

The bad news is there are many members who do not have the spiritual or temporal health they would like, and they frequently wonder why. Often, they *keep the don'ts* and expect to receive the blessings of health but don't realize there are more variables to the formula. Many times they think there is nothing they can do to improve, that they are victims of genetics or environment, or that they are destined to have the problems they do. They may even wonder if there is something wrong with them that keeps the Lord from blessing them.

Invariably, if they make an improvement in living one of the variables on the left side of the Word of Wisdom Formula, they see their spiritual and physical health improve. Positive changes in another variable may bring even more blessings. When they understand the law, they can better understand how to receive the blessings. In D&C 130:20-21 we read:

20 There is a law, irrevocably decreed in heaven before the foundations of this world, upon which all blessings are predicated.

21 And when we obtain any blessing from God, it is by obedience to that law upon which it is predicated.

Elder A. Theodore Tuttle says, this verse "... *sets forth unmistakably the fact that there are principles upon which promises are predicated, and that obedience is the key to receiving blessings*" (Tuttle 1978).

The better we understand and live the Lord's Law of Health, the greater the likelihood we will receive the promised spiritual and temporal blessings. The greater our knowledge, desire, and capacity are to *keep the don'ts, do the do's,* and *obey the commandments*, then the greater our faith and confidence can be that Heavenly Father will bless us with His promised blessings.

A PERSONAL JOURNEY

In 1979 my wife, Debi, and I understood the *don'ts* of the Word of Wisdom and lived by that principle. Like most members, that was basically all we knew about it. Then we had an experience that gave us new insight and a much greater appreciation for the Lord's Law of Health.

Shortly after we began chiropractic college, Debi broke out in a rash all over her body. We took her into the clinic at the college to see if we could get some help. Several interns looked at her and offered a variety of diagnoses. A doctor happened to be visiting the school that day, and someone invited him into the room to get his opinion. He looked at Debi and said, *"You have a toxic liver. Eat three grapefruits a day for three days, and you will be fine."*

We were startled at his diagnosis of toxic liver. What does a liver have to do with a skin rash? What does it mean to be toxic? We didn't understand what the doctor was talking about. However, we did understand *"eat three grapefruits a day for three days,"* so that is what Debi did. In three days her rash was gone, and it never returned. That was our introduction to nutrition and to the concept that the food we eat has a significant impact on our bodies. What we eat does make a difference!

As a result of this experience, I began a serious study of nutrition and its impact on health. It soon became apparent that there was a great deal of conflicting information on nutrition (a fact that still exists more than thirty years later). I needed a guideline so I could compare the things I was learning to a standard that was true. Without that guideline, I wouldn't know how to interpret the contradictory information I encountered.

Many years ago, I attended a two day seminar on nutrition that I expected would extol the virtues of fruits, vegetables, and whole grains. I was surprised when scientific study after scientific study was projected on the screen showing the importance of consuming large amounts of protein. According to the presenter, one should be eating meat three times a day. Was his presentation with its supporting science correct? Was it really the way to eat in order to be healthy? Without a standard to go by, how could I know?

Because of my faith and my testimony in the restored gospel, I turned to the Word of Wisdom for answers. This revelation became a standard to guide me through a jungle of nutritional information. In eight short verses the Lord outlines nutritional principles, that if adhered to, bring promised blessings of health. These verses quickly became my guiding light to determine what is and what is not beneficial for us to consume.

However, I soon learned that there was even more to the Word of Wisdom than the don'ts and the do's. Patients, like Tom with his back problem, were able to heal and get well when they dealt with the stresses of life by *"walking in obedience to the commandments."* Miracles occurred when gospel principles like forgiveness were applied.

For more than 30 years this Word of Wisdom Formula has served me well personally, in my family, and in a clinical setting. I have learned that those who follow it, no matter what the current trends, fads, or science may say, are much more likely to retain or regain their health.

THE WORD OF WISDOM SOLUTION

If you suffer from fatigue, chronic pain, blood sugar problems, overweight, high blood pressure, inability to sleep, depression or numerous other ailments or conditions and want to *"have health in the navel and marrow in the bones...and run and not be weary and walk and not faint" (D&C 89: 18, 20),* then the principles contained in the Word of Wisdom are the solution.

If you want *"...wisdom and great treasures of knowledge, even hidden treasures"* (D&C 89:19), specifically in relation to health concerns you may have, then my hope is that this book will enlighten you and encourage you in your efforts to seek personal revelation to solve these concerns.

President Ezra Taft Benson taught, *"The Word of Wisdom allows us to know that the Lord is vitally concerned about the health of His Saints. He has graciously given us counsel for improving our health, endurance, and resistance to many diseases"* (Benson, Ezra Taft 1983).

President Boyd K. Packer added, *"The Word of Wisdom does not promise you perfect health, but it teaches how to keep the body you were born with in the best condition and your mind alert to delicate spiritual promptings"* (Packer 1996).

The counsel of these two apostles is the framework for this book. By following the Word of Wisdom more closely, you can improve your health, endurance, and resistance to disease. You can know how to keep your body in its best condition and most importantly, keep your mind alert to spiritual promptings. What wonderful and remarkable promises are yours as you give heed to this marvelous revelation!

This book is divided into three parts according to the three principles that you need to follow to receive the promised blessings. Remember to look at these principles as *variables* to remind you that your willingness and ability to keep these principles, as well as the blessings you receive, *vary* according to your application, understanding, desires, and faith.

PART 1 .... VARIABLE K = KEEPING THE DON'TS.

PART 2 .... VARIABLE D = DOING THE DO'S.

PART 3 .... VARIABLE O = OBEDIENCE TO THE COMMANDMENTS.

As you better align yourself with these three variables, your health will improve and you will receive more temporal and spiritual blessings in your life.

Part 1

THE "K" VARIABLE
KEEPING THE DON'TS

2

KEEPING THE DON'TS

Joy was having terrible behavioral problems with her six-year-old daughter. Talley was obnoxious, defiant, belligerent, and mean. She needed a special aide to be with her at all times in her kindergarten classroom. The problem started when she was two years old and kept getting worse. She didn't grow out of the "terrible twos" like Joy had hoped. Doctors had tried different medications, but Talley reacted adversely to them. They only made her behavior more aggressive. Then Joy made a discovery. She learned of a *"don't"* that significantly improved Talley's behavior.

SPECIFIC DON'TS OF THE WORD OF WISDOM

We all know the specific *don'ts* included in the Word of Wisdom. They have been taught to us since a very young age or since we began to investigate the teachings of the Church. Summarized, they are:

<u>**D&C 89:7-9**</u>
7 Strong drinks (alcoholic or harmful beverages) are not for the belly.
8 Tobacco is not for the body ... and is not good for man.

17

9 Hot drinks (defined as tea and coffee) are not for the body or belly.

Those specifics have stayed the same since Joseph Smith received the revelation in 1833, but Church officials also counsel us against other addictive substances. The Church Handbook of Instructions states,

"The only official interpretation of 'hot drinks' (D&C 89:9) in the Word of Wisdom is the statement made by early Church leaders that the term 'hot drinks' means tea and coffee. Members should not use any substance that contains illegal drugs. Nor should members use harmful or habit-forming substances except under the care of a competent physician" (Handbook 2: Administering the Church 2010).

A little more specific counsel is given to the youth by the First Presidency in the *For the Strength of Youth* pamphlet.

"Avoid any drink, drug, chemical, or dangerous practice that is used to produce a "high" or other artificial effect that may harm your body or mind. Some of these include marijuana, hard drugs, prescription or over-the-counter medications that are abused, and household chemicals. Use of these substances can lead to addiction and can destroy your mind and your body" (For the Strength of Youth 2011).

Darwin's Experience

"I know I do better when I follow the Word of Wisdom. I went skiing two weeks ago, and skied really hard the first day, as I always do. For the past twenty years, since I was fifteen, I have done that and have always been extremely stiff and sore the second day. This time I ate lots of fruit and drank lots of water after skiing that first day. I didn't drink any alcohol or eat any junk. The second day I was hardly stiff at all. I couldn't believe how good I felt! I skied just as I hard as I did the first day. It really makes a difference."

These don'ts are generally well understood by members of the Church. They have been emphasized much more than the do's and adherence to them is expected. Huge volumes of research and life experience now give credence to their validity. With so many choices in our world today, some people may wish for more specific instruction on what they should abstain from. However, Elder Packer taught,

"Members write in asking if this thing or that is against the Word of Wisdom. It's well known that tea, coffee, liquor, and tobacco are against it. It has not been spelled out in more detail. Rather, we teach the principle together with the promised blessings. There are many habit-forming, addictive things that one can drink or chew or inhale or inject which injure both body and spirit which are not mentioned in the revelation" (D&C 58:26) (Packer 1996).

Elder Packer says it is the principle behind the Lord's Law of Health that we need to emphasize. That is what brings the promised blessings. *"The Word of Wisdom was 'given for a principle with promise' (D&C 89:3). That word principle in the revelation is a very important one. A principle is an enduring truth, a law, a rule you can adopt to guide you in making decisions. Generally principles are not spelled out in detail. That leaves you free to find your way with an enduring truth, a principle, as your anchor"* (Packer 1996).

Keeping the don'ts is more than abstaining from tea, coffee, tobacco, and alcohol. It is an important principle that guides us in recognizing what is not good for us to consume.

THE PRINCIPLE IS MOST IMPORTANT

It is this guiding principle that allowed Joy to discover the *"don't"* that affected her daughter. Joy observed that Talley had been doing particularly well one day when, for no apparent reason, her behavior suddenly became worse. It was like someone had flipped a switch. Talley became very aggressive and started throwing things. About thirty minutes previous to this incident Talley had consumed a strawberry soda, and Joy wondered if this might be a trigger. The next time Talley was having a good day Joy gave her another strawberry soda. Within thirty minutes, Talley suddenly blew up. Once again she became violent. After more experimentation, Joy figured out that the major culprit causing Talley's aggressive behavior was the food dye in the soda. She experimented with other foods containing dyes, like flavored corn chips and popsicles, and found the same reaction. Joy discovered that all food dyes made Talley more violent, but red was the worst. It was not easy, but by limiting Talley's consumption of foods with dyes in them, Talley's behavior significantly improved.

PERSONAL DON'TS OF THE WORD OF WISDOM

Could something we eat or don't eat really make such a big difference in how our body responds? Yes. Food dyes are not listed in the don'ts of the Word of Wisdom, yet in Talley's case, they were definitely not good for her. President Joseph Fielding Smith was asked why the Lord does not give us further revelation to cover the many other stimulants and drinks that may be harmful to us. His reply was,

"The answer is because such revelation is unnecessary. The Word of Wisdom is a basic law. It points the way and gives us ample instruction in regard to both food and drink, good for the body and also detrimental. If we sincerely follow what is written **with the aid of the Spirit of the Lord,** *we need no further counsel... Thus by keeping the commandment we are promised inspiration and the guidance of the Spirit of the Lord through which we will know what is good and what is bad for the body, without the Lord's presenting us with a detailed list separating the good things from the bad that we may be protected"* (Smith 1957).

In addition to seeking help from health care providers, Joy had spent a great deal of time in prayer over Talley's behavior, seeking the Lord's help in finding a solution. When the thought came to her that her daughter was possibly reacting to the soda, Joy recognized it as an inspired thought. Not only did she find an answer to Talley's problem through prayer, she experienced the greater spiritual blessing offered by the Word of Wisdom to *"find wisdom and great treasures of knowledge, even hidden treasures"* (D&C 89:19). For Talley and her family, the wisdom Joy received was indeed a treasured solution, one that had been hidden for four frustrating years.

Joy and Talley learned that the Word of Wisdom can be very personal. They discovered that Heavenly Father had answers for their particular questions about health, nutrition, and behavior. They came to understand that for Talley, food dyes are a *don't,* and that Talley's K Variable, *Keeping the Don'ts,* includes more don'ts than are specifically listed in the Word of Wisdom.

When we see the Word of Wisdom as a principle of faith that invites revelation more than a list of don'ts, it takes on a new light. We see it as a tool to lead us, guide us, and give us answers rather than being a law that is restrictive and binding. It allows our minds to expand and see options and solutions. Like Joy we can find solutions to health and many other challenges that may concern us.

> ## Reba's Personal Don't
> "I suffer big time from MSG consumption. If I eat food that has MSG in it I get a migraine that will last 2 days. It took me years to discover that MSG, that is hidden in so many things, was the cause."

CONSPIRING MEN

It is important to note the protective reason the Lord revealed this remarkable Principle in the first place.

> **D&C 89:4 ... In consequence of evils and designs which do and will exist in the hearts of conspiring men in the last days, I have warned you, and forewarn you, by giving unto you this word of wisdom by revelation—**

The Word of Wisdom warns us how conspiring men in the last days will try to take advantage of us. President Joseph Fielding Smith described one way this has happened,

"One passage in this revelation (D&C 89:4) is quite generally overlooked. It states that the time should come when wicked and designing men would resort to practices of adulteration of foods and drinks in order to get gain, to the

injury of the health of their victims. How true these words have been. So evil have these practices become that the government was forced to enact pure food and drug laws for the protection of the people" (Smith 1957).

So how does this relate to Joy and Talley? Could evil and designing men be behind the manufacturing and marketing of food dyes? That seems like a silly question, yet to Talley and her family, her reactions to the chemicals could make them wonder.

Thankfully, it's not our job to try to figure out what goes on in the hearts of men. It is the Lord's. Our job is to use the tools Heavenly Father has armed us with so we can discern what is right for us. Obedience to the Word of Wisdom is our answer, but we must understand there are variables.

WHAT ONE PERSON CAN HANDLE, ANOTHER MAY NOT

When it comes to food and drink, something that is good for one person may not be good for someone else. President Joseph Fielding Smith said, *"Some persons are allergic to one thing and others to another, yet what they cannot take are wholesome to others... According to the promise of the Lord we will have wisdom to understand these things by virtue of faithful observance of this basic law—the Word of Wisdom"* (Smith 1957).

Take Rebecca for instance. She reacts to sugar. Sugar is not listed in the Word of Wisdom, but Rebecca has learned she can't handle it. She says she reacts to it like a drug. Like Talley, Rebecca has had spiritual help in figuring this out and overcoming it. Sugar is on her personal list of don'ts.

"Even though my sugar addiction is not specifically mentioned in the Word of Wisdom, I have to pretend it is. It is a reality for me. I have given up smoking, drinking, and drugs. Giving up sugar has been by far the hardest, because you have to eat, and because sugar is added to almost every food you buy. It is extremely difficult to avoid.

"Looking back over my childhood I am now able to realize that my addiction to sugar started early. I thrived on pancakes and syrup, loved desserts, cookies, and goodies of every kind. I turned to sweets on almost a daily basis for years.

22

Eventually I became aware of the harm this was to my health, so I started on a journey to lose weight and become healthy. I was extremely strict with my plan for 5 months losing 55 pounds.

"When Easter weekend came around, I felt it would be okay to have a 'cheat' day, but I completely fell off my healthy bandwagon and went on a sugar craze. I ate every piece of candy or sweet I could find. I could not stop! I was hiding so I could eat sugar and even stayed up late shoving as much junk in my mouth as I could before bedtime, because I knew I would be going back on my weight loss plan the next day.

"My 'restart' day to my diet never came. I was addicted to sugar and refused to let go! I was a beast to everyone and didn't care because eating sugar was more important.

"One day, one of the kids came in while I was in the middle of one of my worst binge sessions. I was inhaling food. I wasn't even enjoying the taste. When my daughter entered, I just lost it! I went crazy and was screaming and yelling like I was a mad woman! How dare she talk to me while I was eating, let alone tell me that what I was eating was not on my diet!

"I sent my daughter to her room and was on my way back to eat more when I called my sister bawling. I told her what had happened, that I had freaked out and was now trying to induce vomiting. I couldn't stop! Who am I?

"I hated me for acting like that. I hated me for gaining weight again. And I hated me for who I was becoming again. I literally believed I was becoming crazy! The guilt was so extremely overwhelming. So were the worthlessness and the despair.

"My sister told me to call my dad and ask for a blessing. I knew it would help, but at the same time I sincerely doubted whether I could give up my addiction!

"I called my dad, and he and mother showed up immediately. I visited with them and told them what was going on, that I was just not doing well. Dad then gave me a priesthood blessing.

"I was told in the blessing that I was a wonderful daughter of God and a good wife and mother. I was actually hearing it as if my Heavenly Father was speaking directly to me. I had never believed nor understood that I was that special. I *know that blessing healed me. The improvement was instant. The self-control, the sugar addiction and cravings and even my doubts were immediately better.*

"I know my family loves me. I can now believe that since I am not in a sugar fog. I am even able to allow that love to grow and become deeper. It's very humbling to have to ask your husband and children to forgive you. However it's worth it!

"My sugar intake is now much less. I haven't quit completely but it is much easier to deal with. I know I can and am able to survive without it. I treat my addiction to sugar as an allergy, and if I do eat it, I eat it sparingly. I know that if I take one bite I will physically crave more. Is that one bite worth it? Not usually.

"I have learned that with Heavenly Father's help, anything is possible!"(Letter in Author's possession 2012).

There are many substances that a person might have a sensitivity or adverse reaction to. With Heavenly Father's help, those can be identified and overcome.

FOODS IN NATURAL STATE ARE BEST

When Joseph Smith received the revelation of the Word of Wisdom, there was little in the way of food additives or other chemicals to be concerned about. Small quantities of sugar and salt were the main ingredients used to enhance flavor and to preserve food. For instance, in 1800, *"the average person consumed about 18 pounds of sugar per year"* (Refined Sugar History 2011). Now it is *"about 150 pounds of sugar per year... or an average intake of about 32 teaspoons of added sugars per person per day"* (Agriculture 2000). That increase of added sugar consumption has been implicated in an increased incidence of diabetes and other diseases. *"In 1893, there were fewer than 3 diabetics per 100,000 people in US. Today, there are 8,000 diabetics per 100,000 people in US"* (Refined Sugar History 2011).

The number of food additives has continued to grow to where there are now well over 12,000 different chemicals added to our foods, mostly for enhanced looks, taste, and preservation. What kind of impact do these chemicals have on our body, individually and collectively? It is hard to say. A single slice of bread may have *"sixteen chemicals in it to keep it feeling fresh"* (Ruth Winter 2004). If we multiply those sixteen chemicals by all the other chemicals we ingest or are exposed to in a day, it would seem logical that they could eventually have some adverse impact upon our health.

President Benson counseled, *"In general, the more food we eat in its natural state and the less it is refined without additives, the healthier it will be for us"* (Benson, Ezra Taft 1974).

What a blessing it is that the Word of Wisdom was given in 1833 as a general principle with a promise! As we apply that principle today to a vastly different set of circumstances than those of the early members of the church, we can still navigate ourselves through the jungle of nutritional do's and don'ts to receive the promised blessings of temporal and spiritual health.

OUR PERSONAL LIST OF DON'TS

Rebecca said that she added sugar "used sparingly" to her personal list of Word of Wisdom Don'ts. Talley has added food dyes to hers. Given the world in which we now live, with all its choices, it is quite likely that all of us need to have a personal list of don'ts in addition to the specific ones listed in the Word of Wisdom. It seems highly unlikely that we are able to receive the blessings of *"health in the navel and marrow in the bones"* and *"run and not be weary and walk and not faint"* without exercising some caution and restraint.

President Joseph Fielding Smith counseled, *"A safe guide to each and all is this: If in doubt as to any food or drink, whether it is good or harmful, let it alone until you have learned the truth in regard to it. If anything offered is habit-forming, we will be safe in concluding that it contains some ingredients that are harmful to the body and should be avoided"* (Smith 1957).

Whether we create that personal list of don'ts through experience or education, Heavenly Father will help guide us in the process through revelation. He will give us *"wisdom and great treasures of knowledge, even hidden treasures"* which we can use to better our health.

SUMMARY: VARIABLE K – KEEPING THE DON'TS

The first variable in the Word of Wisdom Formula is *keeping the don'ts.* In order to receive the promised temporal and spiritual blessings we need to:

1. Abstain from the specific don'ts of tea, coffee, tobacco, alcohol, and illegal drugs.
2. Abstain from personal don'ts revealed by experience, study, and through the Spirit.

THE WORD OF WISDOM FORMULA			
KEEP THE DON'TS	+ DO THE DO'S	+ OBEDIENCE TO COMMANDMENTS	= PROMISED BLESSINGS

Part 2

THE "D" VARIABLE
DOING THE DO'S

3

DOING THE DO'S

Bruce decided it was time to take up running again. It had been two years since he last ran, and he felt like it was time for him to get back into shape. During that time he had also changed his diet: giving up soda pop; cutting way back on sweets, meats, and processed foods; and eating significantly more fruits and vegetables. He decided not to push himself as he began running, but to just take it easy. He thought a fifteen minute run would be plenty. After fifteen minutes, he still felt very fresh and decided to run further. He ran another fifteen minutes and still felt great. Bruce continued to run, and run, amazed at how well he felt. After six miles he finally stopped because he was concerned about how stiff and sore he would be the next day, not because he needed to. To his surprise, he woke up feeling fine with hardly any stiffness or soreness at all. He attributed this difference from what he expected to his new way of eating.

Bruce had never used any of the don'ts mentioned in the Word of Wisdom. He was an active member of the Church and recognized both the spiritual and physical harm they caused. But he also had never really paid any attention to the do's. Like most members of the Church, he had a vague idea of what they were but made no connection between them and his health. After his six mile run, the promise *"run and not be weary and walk and not faint"* took on a new meaning for him. He discovered that it was literally true. Having done a fair bit of running in the past, this experience was life changing for Bruce. He had discovered a secret in the Word of Wisdom that brought him more endurance than anything else he had previously experienced.

THE 4 FOOD GROUPS OF THE WORD OF WISDOM

What are the "do's" of the Word of Wisdom? What are the foods the Lord tells us to eat? They are outlined very simply in eight concise verses.

D&C 89:10-17

10 And again, verily I say unto you, all wholesome herbs God hath ordained for the constitution, nature, and use of man—

11 Every herb in the season thereof, and every fruit in the season thereof; all these to be used with prudence and thanksgiving.

12 Yea, flesh also of beasts and of the fowls of the air, I, the Lord, have ordained for the use of man with thanksgiving; nevertheless they are to be used sparingly;

13 And it is pleasing unto me that they should not be used, only in times of winter, or of cold, or famine.

14 All grain is ordained for the use of man and of beasts, to be the staff of life, not only for man but for the beasts of the field, and the fowls of heaven, and all wild animals that run or creep on the earth;

15 And these hath God made for the use of man only in times of famine and excess of hunger.

16 All grain is good for the food of man; as also the fruit of the vine; that which yieldeth fruit, whether in the ground or above the ground—

17 Nevertheless, wheat for man, and corn for the ox, and oats for the horse, and rye for the fowls and for swine, and for all beasts of the field, and barley for all useful animals, and for mild drinks, as also other grain.

If we look carefully and combine the verses a little, we can see that these do's can be divided into **4 Food Groups**. They are:

1. Herbs (footnote says "Plants") – "All wholesome herbs (plants)… every herb (plant) in the season thereof" (Verses 10-11).

2. Fruit – "Every fruit in the season thereof… the fruit of the vine; that which yieldeth fruit, whether in the ground or above the ground" (Verse 11, 16).

3. Flesh – "Flesh also of beasts and of the fowls of the air... to be used sparingly... only in times of winter, or cold, or famine... and excess of hunger" (Verses 12-13, 15).

4. Grain – "All grain is ordained for the use of man... to be the staff of life… all grain is good for the food of man… nevertheless, wheat for man... barley... for mild drinks, as also other grain" (Verses 14, 16-17).

President Ezra Taft Benson taught that our physical health influences our spirit. In a BYU devotional he said, *"There is no question that the health of the body affects the spirit, or the Lord would never have revealed the Word of Wisdom. God has never given any temporal commandments--that which affects our stature affects our soul. There are at least four basic areas which make the difference in your health--in your growing in stature"* (Benson, Ezra Taft 1979).

President Benson said that the four basic areas that affect our health are righteousness, food, exercise, and sleep. He emphasized food and what we should eat by saying, *"To a great extent we are physically what we eat. Most of us are acquainted with some of the prohibitions (of the Word of Wisdom), such as no tea, coffee, tobacco, or alcohol. What need additional emphasis are the positive aspects--the need for vegetables, fruits, and grains, particularly wheat"* (1979).

He did not stop with foods we should emphasize in our diets, but also issued a caution, *"In most cases, the closer these (foods) can be, when eaten, to their natural state--without over-refinement and processing--the healthier we will be. To a significant degree, we are an overfed and undernourished nation digging an early grave with our teeth, and lacking the energy that could be ours because we overindulge in junk foods"* (1979).

Bruce experienced what President Benson taught. He

replaced much of the refined and processed foods he was eating with whole foods and experienced a stronger and healthier stature. As a result, he *"could run and not be weary and walk and not faint."*

Brenda is another individual who came to understand the blessing of improved health by doing the do's of the Word of Wisdom. Brenda and her husband had five children. Their children were "always" sick and medical bills consumed a significant part of the family budget. When Brenda first learned about the do's of the Word of Wisdom, she re-read the commandment and gained great insight. She had been good about keeping the don'ts but doing the do's was a new concept to her. Her family ate fruit occasionally, very few vegetables if any, and lots of meat, dairy products, and refined wheat flour foods. She decided it would be worth it to try to alter their diets. It took a great deal of effort on Brenda's part, but she was able to change her family's diet. Within a year, the health of the entire family had significantly improved. From then on they had very few medical bills due to illness. Brenda attributed it to following the do's in the Word of Wisdom.

NUTRITION – A CONFUSING SCIENCE

Many books and articles have been written on the subject of nutrition. We can hardly pick up a magazine without reading a headline extolling the latest weight loss or nutrition fad. Much of what is written is conflicting and contradictory. Even an in-depth study can leave us totally confused. There is research, science, opinions, and beliefs that back almost every diet imaginable, but that is not the only confusing thing. We only need to go to another part of the world and observe some of the foods eaten there to question some of our own dietetic ideas. What we consider a staple and necessary part of a healthy diet may not even exist there. It is all very confusing.

When the don'ts were revealed on February 27, 1833, there was little science to support them. Huge volumes of research now give credence to their validity. There was even less scientific evidence in 1833 to support nutritional recommendations. One of the few observations that had been made was that sailors often came down with scurvy and fruit seemed to prevent it. As a result, in 1795 the British Navy issued limes for sailors so they wouldn't get the disease. It wasn't until 125 years later that the cause of scurvy was discovered, a deficiency of Vitamin C (Vitamin C History 2012).

Much has changed since 1833. We now know much more about food and how it affects the body and contributes to health. But sadly, the science is still very confusing, or at least the interpretation and application of it is. I reviewed a book where the author states, *"I tell my patients fruit is a poison... and I mean it when I say, don't eat it!"* (Carlson, James 2007). Dr. Carlson is a well-studied and highly educated man. He wrote his book in an effort to share the scientific knowledge he has gained that enables a person to avoid disease, to heal, and be well. He has had a tremendous amount of success with patients in his clinic who follow his nutritional recommendations.

In contrast to Dr. Carlson's statement, Dr. Joel Fuhrman, another author and researcher claims, *"Fruit is an essential part of our diets. It is an indispensable requirement for us to maintain a high level of health"* (Fuhrman, Joel 2003). In fact Dr. Fuhrman suggests we should eat at least four pieces of fresh fruit a day (p 181). Dr. Fuhrman is also a very well-studied and highly educated physician. His patients also experience remarkable improvements in their health when they follow his recommendations.

These types of statements and recommendations are confusing. Does it really matter what we eat? The contradicting ideas would seem to suggest not, yet science still says it does. The increasing incidence of obesity, poor health, and chronic disease in America has been linked study after study to what we eat (Must 1999). Seven of ten Americans die from chronic diseases *"that are almost entirely the result of decades of unhealthy living"* (Aldana, Steven 2005).

But which study do we believe? Without some sort of standard we are left to wonder. Do we eat lots of fruit or not any fruit... lots of protein or a little protein... high fat foods or low fat foods... lots of carbohydrates or few carbohydrates? Are starches good or bad? Do we take supplements or not, and if so, which ones? Is butter or margarine better? Do we really need to use olive oil or take fish oil? Are eggs good or bad? Is milk a health food or not? Is sugar better than artificial sweeteners or vice versa? What's the difference between fresh, canned, frozen, and dried foods? Between whole grains and refined grains? What about juices, soda pop, sports drinks, and energy drinks? How about preservatives, flavor enhancers, food dyes, texturizers, and other food additives? Should we follow some specific diet related to genetics, blood type, disease, aging, weight loss, etc.? There are well over 300 such diets to choose from (Diet Index 2012).

THE WORD OF WISDOM – A TRUE STANDARD

In the Word of Wisdom we have a standard to which we can compare other nutritional information and advice. We have a revealed promise that yields temporal and spiritual blessings when we adhere to it. When we read an article or a study on nutrition, we can hold it up in the light of the Word of Wisdom to see how much credit we want to give it. If it fits our standard, then we can incorporate what it says or the parts of it that do fit into our diet. If it doesn't fit our standard, then we can ignore it. We are not saying that the study is incorrect or that the article is not true. We may not have the knowledge or insight to determine that. We are simply saying that it doesn't fit our protocol and our approach to receiving the promised blessings.

In the next four chapters we will look at each of the 4 Food Groups of the Word of Wisdom. We will look at science that supports them, comments from general authorities, and supporting scriptures. We will look at why this commandment, given 180 years ago, is still so true and powerful today. Hopefully your knowledge, faith, and understanding of this remarkable commandment will be enhanced so you can receive more of the spiritual blessings and the promised blessings of health.

4

THE 4 FOOD GROUPS – HERBS (PLANTS)

William was thirty-one years old and said he felt like he was ninety. He was experiencing fatigue, memory loss, slurred speech, and had a difficult time putting a sentence together. For twelve years he had suffered weekly migraines. For nine years he had dealt with burning and numbness in his arms and hands as well as pain in all his joints that was often disabling. Eight months earlier, periods of forgetfulness began. For three months he had been having episodes where he would "blank out" and become unresponsive. He had not been able to work for two weeks because of pain and weakness in his legs, and he was not even able to walk on his own. One day he passed out and was transported to the hospital emergency room where an MRI and other tests ruled out a brain tumor. Medications and other treatments William had tried over the years had offered some relief, but he was continually getting worse.

William's typical menu was cold cereal for breakfast, processed meat and white bread sandwiches for lunch, and a steak and baked potato for supper. He didn't eat any other vegetables and maybe had one piece of fruit a week. He drank very little water and several cups of coffee a day (though not the thirty-six a day he used to drink in college).

William learned about the don'ts and do's of the Word of Wisdom and decided it was worth a try to see if nutritional changes would make a difference in his health. He cut back on his coffee, added two fruits, two vegetables and plenty of water to his daily diet. Within a week he was no longer blanking out or experiencing memory loss, and was able to return to work for four hours a day. Within two weeks William was back to work full time, had much more energy, and had no more pain, numbness, or burning. William continued to make improvements in his diet according to the principles he had learned and within six weeks felt like a thirty-one year old should feel.

How did a change in William's diet make him feel so much better and cause such a huge improvement in his health? Undoubtedly, cutting back on coffee helped, but it is also important to understand the role that fruits and vegetables played in his self-healing. Let's start with the first Food Group of the Word of Wisdom – Herbs.

FOOD GROUP 1 – HERBS (VEGETABLES, LEGUMES)

"All wholesome herbs God hath ordained for the constitution, nature, and use of man... every herb in the season thereof" (D&C 89:10-11).

The footnote reference to verse 10 says that herbs are **plants**. Elder John A. Widstoe defined "herbs" this way, *"The word "herb" was frequently used a century ago to include plants and vegetables, direct products of the soil. The dictionary defines it to be: 'a plant that dies completely, or down to the ground, after flowering'. Also 'an herbaceous plant used medicinally'. As used in the Word of Wisdom it was undoubtedly meant to include all plants the use of which is good for man. The modifying words 'all wholesome' indicate that all edible vegetables and fruits of earth are included in the term; they also indicate that some 'herbs' are not fitted to be used as food"* (Widstoe 1937).

In our day we tend to think of herbs only in a medicinal way, but as Elder Widstoe says, wholesome herbs are also edible plants that grow in or on the ground, like vegetables. Legumes, such as soybeans and lentils, would also seem to fit into this category, so I will include them here. Fruits will be discussed in the next chapter.

FUNCTION OF FOODS

Before we talk about the specifics of why we need to eat vegetables and legumes, we need to make sure that we understand the important role that food plays in our body. There are 3 important functions.

1. **Build and Repair Tissues** – Food is needed to provide the energy and supply the materials to grow the body and fix the wear and tear that comes from daily living. Approximately 60 to 75% of the energy derived from the food we eat is used for this bodily maintenance (Insel, Paul 2011).

2. **Maintain Body Temperature** – Similar to burning wood in a campfire to keep warm, food is burned as fuel to keep the body's temperature at 98.6° F. This requires about 10% of the energy derived from the food we eat (Insel, Paul 2011). However, that would obviously be more during the winter when we are out in the cold and less during the summer when it's 100° F. As evidence, consider that in the winter we naturally crave more calorie dense foods, which provide more energy, like steak, stew, or oatmeal. We crave less calorie dense foods in the summer like salads, cucumbers, or watermelon. Eating a steak is like throwing a big log on the fire and eating watermelon is like tossing on a few tiny twigs. Watermelon when it's -20° F is not appealing at all, but watermelon on a hot summer day is refreshing.

3. **Furnish Energy for Physical Work** – The third function of food is to provide the energy to perform our daily labors. Exercise, work, play and in fact any movement, account for 15 to 30% of total energy expenditure (Insel, Paul 2011).

COMPONENTS OF FOOD

So food provides two basic products - **Fuels** for our body to give us energy and **Materials** with which our body can build and repair itself and perform its various functions. There are six components of food that provide these two products. They are carbohydrates, fats, proteins, nutrients, fiber and water. They are used in the body as follows:

FUELS	MATERIALS
1. Carbohydrates - main fuel	1. Protein - for growth and repair
2. Fats – reserve fuel	2. Nutrients – vitamins, minerals, fatty acids, and phytonutrients for proper body function
3. Proteins – backup fuel	3. Fiber – for proper digestion
	4. Water – for transportation of nutrients and wastes

Of the three fuels, carbohydrates are the main fuel our body uses to supply us with energy and body heat. When there are not enough carbohydrates available, fats are a reserve fuel that the body can turn to for energy. In addition protein, which is on both lists, can also be burned as a backup fuel, but the main purpose of protein is growth and repair. Of the rest of the materials, nutrients like vitamins, minerals, and other similar chemicals are necessary for proper functioning of the body and for good health. Fiber is necessary to keep digestion working smoothly, and water is vitally important for proper functioning of the entire body. The foods we eat should contain good quality fuels and adequate materials so our body can function optimally.

HOW FOODS ARE USED

Let's compare the body to a house so we can get a more familiar idea of the role these food components play in our body. (We will make it an electric house so the fuel for heating, cooling and powering appliances is all the same – electricity.) This will be an overview of what these fuels and materials do, and the foods we find them in. I will go into more detail later.

38

FOOD COMPONENT	EQUIVALENT IN HOUSE
1. Carbohydrates	1. Main Fuel (Electricity)
2. Fats	2. Reserve Fuel (Fireplace)
3. Proteins	3. Structure and Furnishings
4. Nutrients	4. Switches
5. Fiber	5. Drains
6. Water	6. Water Supply (Pipes)

1. **Carbohydrates** - are the chief source of energy in our diet. They are like the electricity used to heat and cool the house and to give power to lights and appliances. They include the starches and sugars of fruits, vegetables, and cereal grains. These starches and sugars are broken down into glucose which is burned by most of the cells in the body to keep up body temperature and provide energy for mental and physical work and for all life processes. Keeping the house at the proper temperature and running electrical devices can consume a large amount of power, and it is the same with our bodies. We need lots of carbohydrates because we need lots of glucose. Carbohydrates are the most abundant and efficient source of fuel we have access to, and they come almost exclusively from plants. Milk is the only animal food that contains carbohydrates (lactose).

2. **Fats** - are energy foods, like carbohydrates, but are more concentrated. They are personal food storage that we carry with us at all times, in case of shortage. Fat is like having a wood burning fireplace as a backup when no electricity is available. Obviously, how much wood we have available to burn depends on the size of the wood pile we have built. Likewise, the amount of fat available as a reserve fuel in the body depends on how much we have stored. Most plant foods have some fat in them, but it is a small amount compared to what is typically found in animal products.

3. **Proteins** - are the body-building foods essential for growth and repair. Muscles, skin, hair, and nails are all made up of proteins. Proteins are like the structure and furnishings of the house, such as lumber, bricks, mortar, shingles, glass, and furniture. Once the house is built, the amount of material necessary to maintain it is relatively small. Likewise, large amounts of protein are not necessary to keep the body well-maintained. Protein is especially concentrated in animal foods like red meat, poultry, fish, eggs, and dairy. Some people have the mistaken notion that it is only animal products that contain protein. However all plant foods are also made of protein, which gives them structure. Even watermelon has protein in it to give it structure or it would fall apart. In our figurative house we have a backup electrical generator in case the power goes out, and we have the same in our body. If there are not enough carbohydrates in our diet, protein can be converted into glucose in our "backup generator" and burned as fuel. However, it is a much more difficult process than converting carbohydrates or fat into glucose.

4. **Nutrients** – such as vitamins, minerals, essential fatty acids, and phytonutrients (health protecting chemicals unique to plants) are required in very small quantities yet are essential for proper functioning of the body. They are like the switches in our house that turn lights, appliances, and other devices on and off. They exert a great deal of influence on what happens in our home. If they are not functioning properly, life can be miserable. Nutrients are necessary for normal growth, good health, and the prevention of disease. Plant foods have the greatest amount and variety of vitamins, minerals, and phytonutrients. Animal foods have concentrated sources of fewer nutrients.

5. **Fiber** – is the indigestible part of plant food that provides the digestive tract with bulk which allows for efficient movement of food through the alimentary canal, especially the large intestine. We want the drains to work well in our house, and the same can be said for our intestines. A sluggish digestive tract can be the source of much discomfort and disease. Fiber is only found in plant foods, not in animal foods.

6. **Water** - forms about 70% of our body weight and is an important constituent of all body cells. It is required for all the biological processes in our body. Water in the body is like the water that flows in the pipes in our house which is necessary for cooking, cleaning, proper hygiene, and sanitation. Losing the water supply can quickly bring the household to a halt, and it can in our bodies also. Water is necessary for blood, digestive juices, and processes of elimination. Water comes from both the plant and animal foods we eat and the water and beverages we drink.

"HERBS" ARE COMPLETE FOODS

Herbs, or edible plants, as defined in the Word of Wisdom, contain all six of these important components of food which means they are complete foods. Let's look at the composition of some common vegetables and legumes to see how they measure up. We will look first at the three Fuel Components of food that supply energy – carbohydrates, fats, and proteins. Then we will look at the Material Components.

The fuel the body uses is measured in terms of calories. A calorie is a term of measurement, like inches or pounds, but rather than measuring length or weight, calories measure the "energy" in food. We can compare it to a log sitting beside the fireplace. There is energy in that log waiting to be released, and when it is put on the fire to burn, the energy is released as heat and warms up the room.

The scientific definition of a calorie is *"the unit of heat*

41

*equal to the **amount** of heat required to raise the temperature of 1 kilogram of water by 1°C at 1 **atmosphere** pressure*" (The American Heritage Dictionary 2012). Practically, this means that when carbohydrates, fats, and proteins are "burned" for fuel, the body has the energy it needs to stay warm and be active. The energy available in carbohydrates and proteins is four calories per gram (consider a gram analogous to the log by the fireplace). Fats are concentrated fuels, and when burned, they yield nine calories per gram, more than twice the amount of carbohydrates and proteins.

Much confusing information about nutrition and health has led people to assume that plant foods only contain carbohydrates, that carbohydrates are bad, and that animal products *must* be eaten to obtain protein and fats (Fuhrman, Joel 2003). This is misleading. The chart below shows the percentage of calories that come from carbohydrates, fats, and proteins in some common vegetables and legumes.

FUEL RATIOS IN VEGETABLES AND LEGUMES				
COMMON FOODS		% Calories from Carbohydrates	% Calories from Fat	% Calories from Proteins
Non-Starchy Vegetables	Spinach	56	14	30
	Broccoli	64	10	26
	Celery	73	10	17
Legumes	Lentils	70	3	27
	Kidney Beans	73	3	24
	Navy Beans	76	4	20
Starchy Vegetables	Carrots	89	5	6
	Potatoes	90	2	8
	Sweet Potatoes	90	1	9

The three foods at the top of the list are considered non-starchy vegetables and are representative of that group of foods. They average about 65% carbohydrates, 10% fat, and 25% protein. As you can see, these foods have a fair amount of protein and fat in them. The middle three foods are representative of legumes and have a higher concentration of carbohydrates and less fat. Their protein content is still quite high, about the same as that of non-starchy vegetables. The last group of foods is starchy vegetables which have the greatest concentration of carbohydrates. They have little fat and a small amount of protein.

Together, these types of foods make up the wholesome herbs talked about in the Word of Wisdom and provide great fuel for our bodies. We should note, however, that though the protein found in these foods could be used for energy production, it will be used for its primary purpose, which is growth and repair. It is much easier on the body to convert carbohydrates to energy than it is to convert protein to energy. Since there are plenty of carbohydrates available, burning protein as fuel is not necessary and does not happen.

ESSENTIAL NUTRIENTS

Producing energy out of food is just one of the amazing functions of the body. There are thousands more performed by this remarkably complex structure of 100 trillion cells, but its overall performance and ability largely depends on the materials it has to work with.

If we build a house, it is important to have a blueprint and the necessary materials with which to build. If we are missing some lumber, or don't have enough nails, or forget to order windows, our new house is going to be less than desirable. Once our house is built, it is always undergoing repairs and maintenance so it's important to have the right materials available. It's also imperative to have the plumbing, drains, switches, etc. in good working order.

It's the same with the body. The body replaces the lining of the stomach about every five days, the skin about every thirty days, the liver about every six weeks, bone cells about every three months, and red blood cells about every four months. The right materials need to be obtainable so the body can rebuild as it should. There are essential nutrients, or materials, the body needs for it to work right. Without them, our health and ability to function falters.

An essential nutrient is one that is "...*necessary for healthy human functioning... and something our bodies cannot make on their own, and therefore must be obtained from an outside source*" (Campbell, T. Colin 2006). These essential nutrients are an important part of the Material Components of food. There are seven of them on which our good health depends: amino acids, vitamins, minerals, fatty acids, fiber, water, and phytonutrients.

1. **Amino Acids** – Proteins are made from chains of amino acids. "*Amino acids serve as the building blocks of proteins... (and) can be linked together in varying sequences to form a vast variety of proteins.*" (Wikipedia 2012) There are twenty amino acids from which all proteins are built, nine of which must be obtained through the food we eat. These nine are called essential amino acids. "*Nine standard amino acids are called "essential" for humans because they cannot be created from other compounds by the human body, and so must be taken in as food*" (Wikipedia 2012).

2. **Vitamins** – These are also essential nutrients that we must obtain from food because the body cannot make them on its own. "*There are 13 vitamins the body needs. They are vitamins A, C, D, E, K and the B vitamins (thiamine, riboflavin, niacin, pantothenic acid, biotin, vitamin B-6, vitamin B-12 and folate)*" (National Institutes of Health 2012). (Note: The body can make 2 of these vitamins if conditions are right: Vitamin D if exposed to sunshine and Vitamin K if beta-carotene is in the food).

3. **Minerals** – There are two kinds of essential minerals we must ingest for good health: macro-minerals and trace minerals. *"Macro-minerals are minerals your body needs in larger amounts. They include calcium, phosphorus, magnesium, sodium, potassium, chloride and sulfur. Your body needs just small amounts of trace minerals. These include iron, manganese, copper, iodine, zinc, cobalt, fluoride and selenium"* (National Institutes of Health 2012).

4. **Essential Fatty Acids** - EFAs are fatty acids required to support the cardiovascular, reproductive, immune, and nervous systems; they are also essential to manufacture and repair cell membranes. *"Only two EFAs are known for humans: alpha-linolenic acid (an omega-3 fatty acid) and linoleic acid (an omega-6 fatty acid)"* (Wikipedia 2012).

5. **Fiber** – Dietary fiber is the indigestible part of plant foods. There are two types:

    a. **Insoluble Fiber:** those that don't dissolve in water. *"This type of fiber promotes the movement of material through your digestive system and increases stool bulk, so it can be of benefit to those who struggle with constipation or irregular stools"* (Mayo Clinic 2012).

    b. **Soluble Fiber:** those that do dissolve in water. *"This type of fiber dissolves in water to form a gel-like material. It can help lower blood cholesterol and glucose levels* (Mayo Clinic 2012).

6. **Water** – Water makes up 60 to 75% of the body weight of the average human being. It forms the bulk of blood and tissue fluid, is essential for transporting nutrients, hormones, and waste products around the body, and also helps control the delicate balances of concentrations within the cells.

7. **Phytonutrients** – These are the newest discoveries. They are chemicals that help promote health and protect against disease but are not yet established as essential nutrients. I am including them here because it's likely that in the future, some of them will be defined as essential nutrients. *"Less than 20% of Americans even know about phytonutrients and their health benefits... Some researchers believe eventually up to 50,000 phytonutrients will eventually be fully cataloged and understood... In the past few decades over 5,000 have been discovered and new ones are being discovered all the time"* (Fee 2011). There are several different categories of phytonutrients and understanding each of them is rather complicated. One simple method is to consider that each color of food represents a different phytonutrient with its own particular health benefits. *"Eating a daily variety of different colors of fruits and vegetables is a convenient way to obtain most of the major phytonutrient classes daily"* (Fee 2011).

Let's look at how these Essential Nutrients measure up in our nine sample foods in the following chart. We are not concerned about quantities of these nutrients at this point, just whether or not the nutrient is present in that specific food. The Perfect Score row shows how many Essential Nutrients exist in that component of food. A perfect score would be 9 amino acids, 13 vitamins, 10 minerals, 2 fatty acids and the presence of fiber, water and phytonutrients.

ESSENTIAL NUTRIENTS IN VEGETABLES AND LEGUMES							
FOOD	Amino Acids	Vitamins	Minerals	Fatty Acids	Fiber	Water	Phyto-nutrients
Perfect Score	**9**	**13**	**10**	**2**	**Yes**	**%**	**Abundant**
Spinach raw (Non-Starchy Vegetables)	9	11	10	2	Yes	91	Abundant
Broccoli raw (Non-Starchy Vegetables)	9	11	10	2	Yes	89	Abundant
Celery raw (Non-Starchy Vegetables)	9	11	10	1	Yes	96	Abundant
Lentils boiled (Legumes)	9	10	9	2	Yes	70	Abundant
Kidney Beans boiled (Legumes)	9	9	9	2	Yes	89	Abundant
Navy Beans boiled (Legumes)	9	9	9	2	Yes	64	Abundant
Carrots raw (Starchy Vegetables)	9	10	10	2	Yes	88	Abundant
Potatoes baked (Starchy Vegetables)	9	10	10	2	Yes	77	Abundant
Sweet Potatoes baked (Starchy Vegetables)	9	10	9	2	Yes	76	Abundant

(Nutrition Data 2012)

It is obvious from the chart that these nine sample foods are all good for us, providing nearly all of the Essential Nutrients our bodies need to function normally and be healthy. They have complete proteins containing all nine essential amino acids, which might come as a surprise. They also contain almost all the necessary vitamins. The two missing in each food are Vitamin D, which can be obtained from sunshine, and Vitamin B12, which can be obtained by occasionally eating animal products. Most contain all the essential minerals and essential fatty acids. They are all high in fiber, water content, and phytonutrients. These are great foods with which to build and maintain our "house."

This chart also shows us that non-starchy vegetables, legumes, and starchy vegetables have a lot in common. Individually, they have nearly all the essential nutrients needed to be complete foods. Collectively, they do have all of them except for the two vitamins mentioned. If we eat one food that is deficient in a vitamin or mineral, we can easily make it up by eating another food that has more of that vitamin or mineral in it. We don't have to keep track. These foods are so complete that a simple variety will provide all the essential nutrients we need. *"Eating a wide variety of raw and conservatively cooked plant foods (such as steamed vegetables) is the only way we can ensure that we get a sufficient amount of these essential health-supporting elements"* (Fuhrman, Joel 2003, 55).

Vegetables give us almost all the nutrients we need just by themselves. When we add fruits, grains, and meat sparingly, with their nutrients, to these "herbs," we have the perfect nutritional formula to create health in the navel and marrow in the bones, to run and not be weary, and to walk and not faint.

> Grace's Story
>
> *"I was experiencing all of the classic symptoms of menopause - hot flashes, irregular periods, night sweats, mood swings, fatigue, memory lapses, dizziness, weight gain, and many others – and I was only 24. I went to a variety of doctors, but still suffered. When I learned about and implemented all the principles of the Word of Wisdom, I was able to completely overcome my symptoms, get off of all prescription and OTC medications, and get on with an energetic and enjoyable life. Now at age 27 I am doing 100% better.*

HEALING ILLNESSES

By being obedient to the Word of Wisdom we can receive the promised blessing of good health. The scriptures also suggest what we should do when we get sick. One of the first solutions is to ask for a priesthood blessing (D&C 42:44, D&C 66:9). A second solution is found in D&C 42:43:

43 And whosoever among you are sick, and have not faith to be healed, but believe, shall be nourished with all tenderness, *with herbs and mild food*, and that not by the hand of an enemy.

Joseph Smith recorded in his journal how he applied this council to himself. On June 14, 1837, he had been sick at home for two days. He wrote, *"I continued to grow worse and worse until my sufferings were excruciating, and although in the midst of it all I felt to rejoice in the salvation of Israel's God, yet I found it expedient to call to my assistance those means which a kind Providence had provided for the restoration of the sick, in connection with the ordinances; and Dr. Levi Richards, at my request, administered to me **herbs and mild food**, and nursed me with all **tenderness and attention**; and my Heavenly Father blessed his administrations to the easing and comforting of my system, for I began to amend in a short time, and in a few days I was able to resume my usual labors"* (Roberts 1904).

The ordinance Joseph is making reference to is undoubtedly the priesthood administration of the sick. The *"means"* which he called to his assistance, which God has provided for the restoration of the sick, are herbs and mild food and being nursed with tenderness and attention.

In the Book of Mormon we also read how plants were used to heal by removing the causes of diseases. In Alma 46:40 we read,

40 And there were some who died with fevers, which at some seasons of the year were very frequent in the land—but not so much so with fevers, because of the *excellent qualities of the many plants and roots* which God had prepared to remove the cause of diseases, to which men were subject by the nature of the climate—

Of course, many years have passed since these scriptures were first written, so in addition to doing what these verses suggest, we also need to use the resources and understanding we have in our day. Elder Dallin H. Oaks taught, *"Latter-day Saints believe in applying the best available scientific knowledge and*

49

techniques. We use nutrition, exercise, and other practices to preserve health, and we enlist the help of healing practitioners, such as physicians and surgeons, to restore health" (Oaks 2010).

Elder Oaks then quoted Brigham Young who said we need to do more than just exercise faith to be healed and that it is inconsistent with our faith if we don't also do our part. *"It appears consistent to me to apply every remedy that comes within the range of my knowledge, and [then] to ask my Father in Heaven ... to sanctify that application to the healing of my body."* (Oaks 2010)

Brigham Young gave further council on how to know which remedies to apply. He told parents how to proceed when their children are sick. With the abundant choices we have today in nutrition and regarding health care treatments, procedures, and therapies, his teaching is probably even more relevant to our day.

"It is the duty of every father and mother to live so that they may have the mind and will of the Lord concerning their duties to their families... and if they are disposed they may have the privilege, for it is God's mind and will that they should know just what to do for them when they are sick... you should administer to them by the laying on of hands and anointing with oil, and give them mild food, and herbs, and medicines that you understand; and if you want the mind and will of God at such a time, get it" (Young 1877).

Brigham Young says that another great gift we have available to help in healing is personal revelation. As we keep the don'ts and obey the do's of the Word of Wisdom while walking in obedience to the commandments, we qualify to receive its spiritual promise. *"But what is the promise?"* asks Elder Boyd K. Packer, *"The promise, of course, is personal revelation"* (Packer 2003). Personal revelation is a wonderful tool to help us make choices and give us insight on our path of healing and good health.

SUMMARY: VARIABLE D – DOING THE DO'S - HERBS

We live in a time where great medical advancements have been made that help heal and save lives. We also have a much greater understanding of just how powerful proper nutrition is in preventing and treating disease and improving and maintaining health. Notwithstanding what we now know, the enduring motherly counsel to *"eat your vegetables,"* attested to by a simple revelation from 1833, is still one of the most powerful things we can do to have good health.

In summary, the second variable in the Word of Wisdom Formula is *doing the do's,* and the First Food Group is Herbs (Plants). In order to receive the promised temporal and spiritual blessings we need to:

1. **Food Group 1 – Herbs -** Eat lots of vegetables and legumes.

THE WORD OF WISDOM FORMULA			
KEEP THE DON'TS	+ DO THE DO'S	+ OBEDIENCE TO COMMANDMENTS	= PROMISED BLESSINGS

5

THE 4 FOOD GROUPS - FRUITS

Mary had suffered several gallbladder attacks and had reluctantly scheduled a date to have her gall bladder removed. She didn't want to have surgery and didn't think there was any other option, until she learned about the do's of the Word of Wisdom. She started eating lots more fruits and vegetables, and less meat and other fatty foods, and her symptoms soon went away. When the day of her surgery was near, she decided to postpone it and see if her new way of eating would continue to make a difference. Mary continued to feel really well and was grateful to discover that her new diet resolved her gall bladder condition. She also discovered that she needed to maintain that diet. Occasionally, she was tempted to eat some of her old favorite foods and she would experience the pain and nausea again. It wasn't easy for Mary to always eat what she knew she should, because she liked those "other" foods, but she knew what she needed to eat to feel well.

Mary learned that knowing what to eat wasn't enough. She had to follow through and control what she ate, or her symptoms would return. No matter how much knowledge we have, if we don't abide by the law that brings the blessing, the blessing can't come. Elder John A. Widstoe said, "*...to abstain from the things forbidden in the Word of Wisdom as injurious to health is not sufficient; it is equally important to partake of foods that build the body properly and meet bodily needs. Men may heed the natural laws of life and live; or they may ignore and pervert them and suffer disease and finally perish. It is so written and has been so proved throughout thousands of years of* *history"* (Widstoe 1937).

It is as important to do the do's of the Word of Wisdom as it is to keep the don'ts, if we want to have good health. We have to give the body the right materials to work with as well as avoid injurious substances.

FOOD GROUP 2 – FRUIT (FRUITS AND NUTS)

"Every fruit in the season thereof... the fruit of the vine; that which yieldeth fruit, whether in the ground or above the ground" (D&C 89:11, 16).

The second group of food we need to partake of is Fruit. In the Fruit Group we include all the foods we normally consider as fruits. Apples, oranges, strawberries, bananas, and peaches are typical examples. We also include nuts, such as almonds, walnuts, pecans, cashews, and hazelnuts, because they are the fruit of a tree. Some foods, like tomatoes and peanuts, could be placed in either this group or the "Herb" group, and you can consider them in whichever group you like. For our purposes, it doesn't make any difference if they overlap.

In the previous chapter we saw how vegetables and legumes contributed important fuel and essential materials to our body. Let's look at three sample fruits and nuts to see how they contribute as well.

FUEL RATIOS IN FRUITS AND NUTS		% Calories from Carbohydrates	% Calories from Fat	% Calories from Proteins
COMMON FOOD		% Calories from Carbohydrates	% Calories from Fat	% Calories from Proteins
Fruits	Apple	95	3	2
	Orange	91	4	5
	Strawberry	85	8	7
Nuts	Almond	15	72	13
	Pecan	8	87	5
	Cashew	23	66	11

(Nutrition Data 2012)

Fruits have a higher concentration of carbohydrates, and nuts have a higher concentration of fat and protein, but once again we see that all three types of fuel are present in each food. If we only eat apples, there might be a concern that we will eventually be deficient in protein or fat. If we eat some almonds, however, plus some spinach, potatoes, and broccoli, any potential deficiency is eliminated.

The same can be said for essential nutrients as seen in the chart below. One food with more nutrients in a certain area will compensate for another food that may have less. Eating whole, unrefined, unprocessed foods is one of the best ways to make sure we are getting adequate fuel and the essential nutrients that our body needs to be healthy.

ESSENTIAL NUTRIENTS IN FRUITS AND NUTS							
COMMON FOOD	Amino Acids	Vitamins	Minerals	Fatty Acids	Fiber	Water	Phyto-nutrients
Perfect Score	9	13	10	2	Yes	%	Abundant
Apple	9	11	7	2	Yes	86	Abundant
Orange	9	9	9	2	Yes	87	Abundant
Strawberry	9	10	10	2	Yes	91	Abundant
Almond	9	8	10	2	Yes	5	Abundant
Pecan	9	10	10	2	Yes	4	Abundant
Cashew	9	8	10	2	Yes	5	Abundant

(Nutrition Data 2012)

CARBOHYDRATES – GOOD OR BAD?

When we talk about fruit, people often worry about its sugar content. They hesitate to eat very much because they're afraid it will make them fat. They have heard that sugar is fattening, and because fruit has sugar in it, they erroneously believe it must be fattening too. They have heard that carbohydrates are "bad," and because fruit contains carbohydrates, they believe fruit is bad too.

They are correct that sugar is fattening, but only if more sugar is consumed than the body needs. It is *excess* sugar that is fattening. However, it is virtually impossible to eat enough fruit to gain weight, for reasons which we will explain. It is eating refined, processed sugars that causes a person to put on weight, not eating whole, unprocessed fruit.

Carbohydrates are chains of glucose (sugar) that are broken down into glucose molecules when digested. These glucose molecules are carried into most of the cells of the body by insulin to be burned as fuel. Insulin is like a hotel maid with a master key helping a guest (glucose) to find his room. She takes glucose to the cell door and unlocks it. If the "room is full," she takes glucose to the next cell and unlocks it. If it is also full she goes to the next cell. Eventually, if she can't find a cell with room for glucose, she takes him to a fat cell. There is always room available there. Glucose is converted to fat and is stored in the fat cell until he is called upon to be burned as fuel. Too often, he is never called upon. Rather, he welcomes several more guests just like himself, and the fat cell grows larger. If this situation persists, and the body's cells remain "full," diabetes, hypertension, dyslipidemia, cardiovascular disease, obesity, and other abnormalities will likely arise. This condition of the body is known as insulin resistance.

Insulin resistance is like you are driving into a town looking for a motel room for the night and finding "No Vacancy" signs posted at every motel you pass. The real problem is not that the motel owners are resisting guests. It's because their rooms are all full and there is *no more room* for guests, so you have to move on to the next town looking for a place to spend the night.

Insulin resistance is more a problem of the cells being too full than our maid, insulin, not being able to do her job of getting insulin into the cells. The average person consumes an over-abundance of refined sugar (150 pounds per year), and there is no more room available in the cells. *"The underlying cause is the high-fat, high-sugar American diet, lack of physical exercise, and resulting obesity"* (McDougall, John A. 2012). Fruit and other whole plant foods, even though they may be high in carbohydrates, are the solution, not the cause of this problem. They provide the body with the nutrients and energy it needs.

THE POWER OF FIBER

Fruits, vegetables, and legumes are all fairly high in carbohydrates, especially fruits and starchy vegetables. Carbohydrates provide both calories and fiber, and fiber makes a huge difference on how much we eat. Let's take apples as an example. Apples are 95% carbohydrates. In the chart below, notice that when apples are processed, the amount of fiber decreases, and the number of calories increases.

COMPARISON OF APPLE PRODUCTS AND FIBER (1 cup servings)					
	Raw Apple	Unsweetened Applesauce	Sweetened Applesauce	Unsweetened Apple Juice	McDonald's Apple Pie
Calories	65	102	167	114	260
Fiber (g)	3.0	2.7	3.0	.5	0
# Servings X # Calories					

(Nutrition Data 2012)

The above products are 1 cup servings (A 1 cup serving of raw apple is equivalent to one small apple). Suppose you were quite hungry and sat down and had one of these for a snack. Think of how much you would eat or drink if you only had that one thing. Do that for each item listed above. Would it be a 1 cup serving, a 2 cup serving, etc.? How much would you eat in order to be "full"? (The bottom line is yours to fill out if you like.)

Now look at how many calories you would have consumed. The applesauce is a more concentrated food because of processing, so though the fiber content is about the same as the raw apple, it has more calories. You would need to eat 2½ small apples to consume about the same number of calories as 1 cup of sweetened applesauce that has added sugar. You would need to eat four apples to get the same number of calories as one McDonald's Apple Pie. The apple pie is very processed, has added sugars, and has all the fiber removed. Out of these five foods, eating the raw apple is definitely the best choice.

THE FULL FACTOR

There is an important point to consider here: why we stop eating. The obvious answer is because we are "full." The stomach is like a balloon. A balloon can be blown up, but there is a limit. The stomach can expand too, from about four cups when empty to about sixteen cups when completely full (Cheng 2000). There are stretch receptors in the stomach that send signals to the brain that say "stop eating, that is enough." It is the volume of food we eat that stretches the stomach and signals an end to eating, not the number of calories consumed. That is why we feel full after eating four apples (260 calories) and are still hungry after eating the McDonald's Apple Pie (260 calories).

Fiber is a great filler of the stomach and diluter of calories. When we eat apples and other plant foods in their raw or moderately cooked state, we *cannot* consume too many calories. It is virtually impossible because the stomach is full before we reach that level. We would have to eat twenty-three small apples in a day to get 1,500 calories, which is a normal number of calories burned by a woman in a day. A man burning 2,000 calories a day would need to eat thirty of them, not something he would likely be able to do.

On the other hand, we could easily eat 6-8 McDonald's Apple Pies in a day to consume an equal number of calories, and still not be full, so we would eat more until the stretch receptors in the stomach stopped us. Thus, we would consume more calories of sugar than burned in a day making it hard for our "maid," insulin, to find an "empty room." The *excess* sugar would be converted to fat and stored in our fat cells. *"The healthiest way to reduce insulin resistance and lower insulin levels is with a diet high in complex carbohydrates and low in fat, and exercise -- this approach corrects the underlying causes of the resistance"* (McDougall, John A. 2012). We need to eat lots of plant foods in their natural or near natural state to stay fit, trim and healthy!

FOOD PROCESSING

Converting an apple into applesauce, apple juice, or apple pie doesn't just affect fiber and calorie content. Processing of apples has also been found to affect phytonutrient content.

"*Apple juice obtained from Jonagold apples by pulping and straight pressing had 10% of the antioxidant activity of fresh apples, while juice obtained after pulp enzyming had only 3% of antioxidant activity*" (Boyer, Jeanelle 2004). In other words, 90% to 97% of antioxidants were removed while turning apples into apple juice. Apple peels contain a majority of the antioxidants when compared to the flesh, so most of the compounds remained in the apple pomace (pulp).

Apples are a widely consumed, rich source of phytochemicals, and epidemiological studies have linked the consumption of apples with reduced risk of some cancers, cardiovascular disease, asthma, and diabetes. "*In the laboratory, apples have been found to have very strong antioxidant activity, inhibit cancer cell proliferation, decrease lipid oxidation, and lower cholesterol. Apples contain a variety of phytochemicals, including quercetin, catechin, phloridzin and chlorogenic acid, all of which are strong antioxidants*" (Boyer, Jeanelle 2004).

Raw apples are a marvelous health food. Regular apple juice you find in the grocery store has lost a great deal of its nutritional value, and is much less beneficial. Of course, the loss of nutrients with processing is not unique to apples. Any food that is processed is going to lose some of its nutritional value. In particular, processes that expose foods to high levels of heat, light, and/or oxygen cause the greatest nutrient loss. The table below compares the typical maximum nutrient losses for common food processing methods.

TYPICAL MAXIMUM NUTRIENT LOSSES (as compared to raw food)				
	Freeze	Dry	Cook	Cook + Drain	Reheat
Vitamins	5%	30-50%	25-50%	35-70%	10-30%
Minerals	0-10%	0%	25-35%	30-55%	0%

(Nutrition Data 2012)

Fresh fruits and vegetables are generally the most nutritious with frozen foods coming in second. "Fresh" produce, however, isn't *always* fresh and doesn't *always* have the most nutrients. Frozen vegetables can sometimes be more nutritious than fresh supermarket produce. *"Fresh vegetables can lose up to 45 percent of important nutrients by the time they reach the dinner table. Time spent in storage, in transportation and sitting on the shelves means it can be more than two weeks from the vegetables being picked to being eaten"* (Poulter 2010). By contrast, produce frozen close to the time of harvest maintains a higher level of many vitamins and other important nutrients.

IN THE SEASON THEREOF

The Word of Wisdom counsels us to use *"Every herb in the season thereof and every fruit in the season thereof"* (D&C 89:11). President Joseph Fielding Smith said, *"Some have stumbled over the meaning of this expression and have argued that grains and fruits should only be used in the season of their growth and when they have ripened. This is not the intent, but any grain or fruit is out of season no matter what part of the year it may be, if it is unfit for use. The apple under the tree bruised and decaying is out of season while the good fruit is waiting to be plucked from the tree"* (Smith, J. F. 1947). Generally, the fresher the fruits and vegetables are, the better they are for us, but tomatoes out of the garden, properly canned at harvest, are still an excellent source of nutrition.

Elder John A. Widtsoe also commented, *"The phrase 'in the season thereof,' referring to fruits and vegetables, has raised much speculation. It indicates simply the superior value of fresh foods as demonstrated by modern science, but does not necessarily prohibit the use of fruits or vegetables out of season if preserved by proper methods."* (Widstoe, 1951)

It's the natural perishability of fruits and vegetables which determine in what season they should mainly be consumed. Potatoes, for example, are good keepers and would be considered a cold or winter season vegetable. Carrots, cabbage, turnips, beets, and most apples are the same. If these fruits and vegetables are stored properly, very few nutrients are lost. Using an apple as an example again, *"...even after 200 days in storage, the total phenolics (phytonutrients) were similar to those at the time of harvest"* (Boyer, Jeanelle 2004). Strawberries, raspberries, lettuce, green beans, peas, spinach, etc. would be considered summer or warm season foods as they do not store well in their fresh form.

The perishability of fruits and vegetables is determined by their enzyme content and activity. Enzymes are what convert a fruit from "green" to ripe and eventually to rotten. Processing food by freezing, drying, or cooking stops the enzymatic action so the food lasts longer. Refrigeration is another process that slows the enzymes down. Though we lose some of the nutrients in processing, we extend the "season" in which those foods can be consumed. Some foods – grains, seeds, nuts and legumes – contain enzyme inhibitors that allow them to be stored much longer than would be possible otherwise, even several decades.

Fruits and vegetables are also meant to be eaten in certain seasons because of their heating or cooling effect on the body. A person eating salads during the winter may find that he can't stay warm since there is very little body energy produced as salad is digested. What he needs to eat instead are the heavier, more calorie dense, starch (concentrated carbohydrates like potatoes and wheat), and protein foods that require more energy to digest. In the process of digestion, more body heat is produced. Just as physical exercise increases body temperature so does eating these heavier foods because your body works harder to digest them. This is known as the *thermic effect of food.*

"The expression "thermic effect of food" is used to describe the energy expended by our bodies in order to consume (bite, chew and swallow) and process (digest, transport, metabolize and store) food. We "expend energy" by burning calories" (The Thermic Effect 2012). Protein requires the most energy to be digested. It is like throwing an extra log on the fire so the fire will be hot enough to burn the protein. Fat takes the least amount of energy while carbohydrates are somewhere in between. *"The thermic effect produced by protein is about 20% to 30% of the energy intake... carbohydrate and fat approximates 5% to 10% and 0% to 5% respectively"* (Kang 2008). We can see that starch and proteins are generally better winter foods, and non-starchy or high water content fruits and vegetables are better summer foods.

Let's look at some common summer and winter foods to

understand better how this works. The following chart shows how many cups of each food it takes to yield 100 calories of energy for the body to burn. Remember that calories come from carbohydrates, fats, and proteins. Up to this point we have only considered the ratio of these fuels in a food. We have not considered the amount. As you can tell from the chart, the amount, or concentration of the fuel, is important.

AMOUNT OF FOOD THAT YIELDS 100 CALORIES (in cups)							
Summer	Non-Starchy Vegetables	Spinach 13 c.	Zucchini 5 c.	Beans 3 c.	Tomato 3 c.	Berries 2 c.	Peaches 2 c.
Winter	Starches and Proteins	Cooked Oatmeal 2/3 c.	Baked Potato 1/2 c.	Kidney Beans 1/2 c.	Chicken Breast 1/3 c.	Roast Beef 1/3 c.	Cheddar Cheese 1/5 c.

(Nutrition Data 2012)

We would need to eat 13 cups of spinach to provide 100 calories of energy for our body. Though spinach has carbohydrates, fats, and proteins, they are not very concentrated because of all the fiber in the spinach. Remember, fiber is a diluter of calories. We only need to eat 1/3 cup of roast beef to get the same number of calories because roast beef doesn't have any fiber.

The Full Factor says we are going to eat until we get full, not until we reach a certain amount of calories. Filling up on winter foods during the winter will keep us warm. Filling up on winter foods during the summer can create excess body heat and cause us to perspire heavily. It is just the opposite with summer foods. We will stay cooler in the summer and colder in the winter because we are not generating as much body heat. Of course we can eat any of these foods any time during the year, but the simple phrase *"every herb in the season thereof and every fruit in the season thereof"* has a lot more meaning when you put nutritional science behind it.

PRUDENCE AND THANKSGIVING

Another thought provoking phrase in the Word of Wisdom referring to herbs and fruits is, *"...all these to be used with prudence and thanksgiving"* (D&C 89:11). In the next verse the Lord indicates that the flesh of beasts and of fowls should also be used with thanksgiving.

President Joseph Fielding Smith expounded on this, *"The Lord has given us all good herbs, fruits, and grains. These are to be the main foods of men, beast, and fowls. But we should not overlook the fact that they are to be used with 'prudence and thanksgiving.' In another revelation (Sec. 59) we are told they are not to be used 'to excess, neither by extortion.' The difficulty with most of the human family, is eating too much, and failing to heed this counsel. There would be less disease and mankind would live longer if all would also heed the counsel of the Lord concerning the use of wholesome foods. Many a man thinks he keeps the Word of Wisdom, who knows only the 'don'ts,' which are but a part of its great meaning"* (Smith, J. F. 1949). Overeating or indulging, even of good foods, is not a prudent thing to do.

We should also be cautious about the various food products we buy. Elder John A. Widstoe wrote, *"A good wholesome diet composed of all nature's food "in season" should be the rule... The prudent mother or provider of food must be intelligent in these matters and not believe all that is told by shrewd advertising whether by radio or the printed page. If she is prudent she knows that 'conspiring men in the last days' have commercial interests at stake and are far more interested in their own pocket-book than in the public health. Her own and her family's health depends upon knowledge of food values, more so today than at any time in the past"* (Widstoe 1937). If shrewd advertising was a concern in 1937, it can only be much more so today. In 1940 the average supermarket carried 3,000 different items (Smith, A. F. 2007). Today, it is about 40,000 (Food Marketing Institute 2011).

Being prudent also implies not getting carried away or becoming extreme in our nutritional ideas. Elder Boyd K. Packer cautioned *"...learn to use moderation and common sense in*

matters of health and nutrition, and particularly in medication.
Avoid being extreme or fanatical or becoming a faddist. For
example, the Word of Wisdom counsels us to eat meat sparingly
(see D&C 89:12). Lest someone become extreme, we are told in
another revelation that 'whoso forbiddeth to [eat meat] is not
ordained of God' (D&C 49:18)" (Packer 1996). Eating food,
with prudence and thanksgiving, protects us and helps us
appreciate that food is truly a gift from God.

ALKALINE ASH AND ACID ASH FOODS

There is another important principle that will help us be
wiser in our food choices. When food is digested in the body, an
ash is produced. This residue is very similar in concept to the ash
that remains after wood is burned. This ash is of three types -
acid, alkaline, or neutral. The body is alkaline, and to keep it that
way, we need to eat mostly alkaline ash foods which are foods
high in alkaline minerals like potassium, magnesium, calcium,
and sodium. If we consume too many acid ash foods, our body
may eventually become too acid. If the cells of the body become
too acid, they will not be able to function or will function poorly,
and eventually disease will result.

This concept was explained 100 years ago by food
scientist, Henry C. Sherman. In 1915 he wrote, *"The presence of*
potassium carbonate (potash) in wood ashes is familiar to
everyone and accounts for the fact that wood ashes are alkaline
or basic. Similarly those parts of plants which are used for food
in the form of fruits and vegetables yield, on burning, a basic or
alkaline ash...capable of neutralizing acids such as the sulfuric
acid produced in the protein metabolism...Thus the
predominance of base-forming elements among the ash
constituents of fruits and vegetables is of great value to the body
in facilitating the maintenance of the normal neutrality of the
blood and tissues" (Sherman 1914). Most fruits and vegetables
leave an alkaline ash when digested. Most foods with higher
concentrations of protein, like meats and grains, yield an acid
ash.

On the following page is a list of some common alkaline
ash and acid ash foods. As you look at the chart, you can easily
notice that the average person consumes much more food from

the acid ash category than the alkaline ash. The acid from these foods is neutralized by alkaline minerals that come from the foods on the alkaline ash side of the chart. *"High-protein foods produce strong inorganic acids, such as nitric, sulfuric, and phosphoric, and also leave acid ash – all of which require alkalizing minerals for neutralization... before they can be eliminated in the urine."* (M. T. Morter 1987)

A person eating too much of the acid ash foods and not enough of the alkaline ash foods can deplete his body of essential, life-sustaining, alkaline minerals. For example, calcium will be taken out of the bone to neutralize excess dietary acid. Research has shown that *"A diet high in acid-ash proteins causes excessive calcium loss... (and) adversely affects bone, unless buffered by the consumption of alkali-rich foods"* (Barzel, Uriel S. 1998).

COMMON ALKALINE ASH FOODS			COMMON ACID ASH FOODS		
Almonds	Cucumber	Oranges	Bacon	Eggs	Plums
Apples	Dates	Parsnips	Barley	Flour,	Pork
Apricots	Figs	Peaches	Beef	white	Prunes
Avocados	Grapefruit	Pears	Blueberries	Flour,	Rice
Bananas	Grapes	Pineapple	Bran,	wheat	Salmon
Beans,	Green	Potatoes,	wheat	Fish	Sardines
dried	beans	sweet	Bran, oat	Honey	Sausage
Beet	Green	Potatoes	Bread,	Lamb	Scallops
greens	peas	Radishes	white	Lentils	Shrimp
Beets	Lemons	Raisins	Bread,	Lobster	Spaghetti
Black-	Lettuce	Raspberries	wheat	Milk,	Squash,
berries	Lima	Rutabagas	Butter	pasteurized	winter
Broccoli	beans	Soy beans	Carob	Macaroni	Sunflower
Cabbage	Limes	Spinach	Cheese	Oatmeal	seeds
Carrots	Milk, raw	Sprouts	Chicken	Oysters	Turkey
Cauliflower	Millet	Strawberries	Cod	Peanut	Veal
Celery	Molasses	Tangerines	Corn	Butter	Walnuts
Chard	Mushroom	Tomatoes	Crackers	Peanuts	Wheat
Cherries	Onions	Watermelon	Cranberries	Peas, dried	Yogurt

(Morter, M.T. 1996)

There are two dangers from eating acid-forming foods too freely. Elder Widstoe identified these, *"First, the kidneys are overworked when required to handle too many of the acid by-*

products of digestion; second, the calcium carbonate of the bones and teeth as well as the basic substances of the tissues are attacked in neutralizing acids that may predominate in the body. Thus, acid-forming foods may in reality rob, not nourish the body" (Widstoe 1937).

Acid ash foods are generally higher in protein because protein is what makes them acid. However, protein is not the only possible source of excess acid in the diet that can rob nutrients from the body. Another food product that yields high levels of acid for the body to dispose of is a cola drink which contains phosphoric acid. This too must be neutralized by minerals. Drinking soda pop, especially colas, is very hard on the body. One possible adverse effect is soreness and cramping when potassium is withdrawn out of the muscles to neutralize the phosphoric acid (Tsimihodimos V. 2009).

The mineral substances necessary for life are mainly available to us through the food which comes directly or indirectly from the plants and fruits of earth. Vegetables, grains, and fruits form nature's storehouse of food minerals. Elder Widstoe emphasized their importance and said, *"From fruits and vegetables should be chosen the bulk of the food in order to keep the body chemically right, for they are important sources of necessary minerals and vitamins"* (Widstoe 1937).

Innumerable scientific studies and personal experiences have demonstrated over and over again the truth of what Joseph

> David's experience
> David had been having leg cramps off and on for two months. Then he broke out in hives. David learned about acid ash foods and how they could rob potassium from the body causing leg cramps and other symptoms. He realized he had been drinking at least a mug of soda pop a day and eating more candy bars and other refined foods. He stopped eating these acid forming foods and started eating lots more alkaline ash foods and drinking water. Within a week his hives and muscle cramps disappeared.

Smith told us in two simple verses in the Word of Wisdom,

10 And again, verily I say unto you, all wholesome herbs God hath ordained for the constitution, nature, and use of man—

11 Every herb in the season thereof, and every fruit in the season thereof; all these to be used with prudence and thanksgiving.

Whether we are dealing with minor pain or serious disease, or just want to maintain good health, fruits and vegetables are an important part of the solution. Dr. Joel Fuhrman who has treated more than 20,000 people in his private clinic with a plant based diet said, *"There is no longer any question about the importance of fruits and vegetables in our diet. The greater the quantity and assortment of fruits and vegetables consumed, the lower the incidence of heart attacks, strokes, and cancer"* (Fuhrman, Joel 2003). Fruits and vegetables should constitute a major portion of our diet if we desire health in the navel and marrow in the bones, and to run and not be weary and to walk and not faint.

SUMMARY: VARIABLE D – DOING THE DO'S - FRUITS
The second variable in the Word of Wisdom Formula is *doing the do's*. Eating foods in the Fruit Food Group is an important *do* that complements the Herbs Food Group. In order to receive the promised temporal and spiritual blessings we need to:

1. **Food Group 1 – Herbs** – Eat lots of vegetables and legumes.
2. **Food Group 2 – Fruits** – Eat lots of fruit and some nuts.

THE WORD OF WISDOM FORMULA			
KEEP THE DON'TS	+ DO THE DO'S	+ OBEDIENCE TO COMMANDMENTS	= PROMISED BLESSINGS

6

THE 4 FOOD GROUPS –
MEAT SPARINGLY

Jonathan had recently taken on a new job in the oil field, so he and his wife had moved their family to a new town and bought a house. They were excited about the prospects of his new employment, but then his gout acted up. Jonathan was 43 years old and had dealt with gout for several years. About six months into his job his symptoms worsened. His ankle swelled up, and he found it impossible to put on his work boot. The pain was severe. Although he was a good worker, he couldn't do his job, so his employer had to lay him off.

Jonathan's favorite food was meat, and he ate a lot of it. He didn't know that symptoms of gout could merely be symptoms of eating too much meat. Gout is caused by excess uric acid in the bloodstream, and one source of uric acid is animal protein. We mentioned in the previous chapter that the digestion of protein yields strong inorganic acids like sulfuric, nitric, and phosphoric. Uric acid is another one of these acid by-products.

Jonathan cut way back on his consumption of meat and began to eat more vegetables even though he wasn't particularly fond of them. He was fond of the results though and within a month was back at work. Jonathan learned that eating foods from the first two food groups of the Word of Wisdom, Herbs and Fruit, put his body back in balance and helped him heal. He also learned that he could not consume as much meat as he had in the past, but why? The answer is in Food Group number three.

FOOD GROUP 3 – MEAT SPARINGLY (MEAT & DAIRY)

"Flesh also of beasts and of the fowls of the air... to be used sparingly... only in times of winter, or cold, or famine... and excess of hunger..." (Verses 12-13, 15).

MEAT – WHY SPARINGLY?

The revelation given in 1833 to eat the flesh of beasts and fowls (or *meat* as we will call it) sparingly was likely just as enlightening to the early church members as abstaining from tobacco. It was thought at the time that eating meat was necessary for strength and hard work. *"In the mid-1800s, popular opinion was that protein was the primary fuel for working muscle"* (Ira Wolinsky 2008). This hypothesis persisted, until the 1900's when scientific research proved that carbohydrates and fats were the main fuels the body used.

An early analytical chemist wrote in 1905 that meat was not necessary for energy, rather, plant foods were. He said, *"Formerly, protein matter was looked upon as the most valuable part of the food, and a large proportion was thought necessary for hard work. It was thought to be required, not only for the construction of the muscle substance, but to be utilized in proportion to muscular exertion.* **These views are now known to be wrong.** *A comparatively small quantity of protein matter, such as is easily obtained from vegetable food, is ample for the general needs of the body. Increased muscular exertion requires but a slight increase of this food constituent. It is the carbohydrates, or carbohydrates and fats that should be eaten in larger quantity, as these are the main source of muscular energy"* (Duncan 1905).

It doesn't take much protein to maintain the body once the "house" is built. Therefore, one reason to eat meat sparingly is because there is no physiological reason to eat large amounts. We can simply obtain all the necessary nutrients from plants.

THE PROBLEM OF EXCESS PROTEIN

Meat contains protein and fat but not carbohydrates. Protein and fat are both essential nutrients, but excess of either can lead to many health issues. Let's look at protein first.

Science tells us that, *"Every day we use about 20 to 30 grams of protein... this is called the 'obligatory loss of protein'"* (M.T. Morter 1996). Replacement of this protein comes from the food we eat, and it doesn't matter whether the source is plants or animals. How much do we need to eat every day to replace the protein lost and to keep the body in good working order? The United States government's established recommended dietary allowance (RDA) is 46 grams a day for women and 56 grams a day for men. (Center for Disease Control 2012) This is twice the obligatory loss of 20 to 30 grams so allows extra protein for situations of greater need.

To better understand what those numbers mean let's look at how much 56 grams is in some sample foods. We will use the summer and winter foods we used in the previous chapter and we will use *cups* for portion size rather than 100 gram portions. For most of us, that is much easier to visualize. The chart below shows how many cups of each food we would need to eat to consume 56 grams of protein, if that food was the only food we ate during the day. For example, if all we ate today was spinach, we would need to eat 62 cups to get 56 grams of protein. If all we ate was roast beef, we would only need to eat 1.3 cups.

AMOUNT OF FOOD THAT YIELDS 56 GRAMS OF PROTEIN (in cups)							
Summer	Non-Starchy Vegetables	Spinach 62 c.	Zucchini 37 c.	Beans 23 c.	Tomato 35 c.	Berries 51 c.	Peaches 40 c.
Winter	Starches and Proteins	Cooked Oatmeal 9.5 c.	Baked Potato 22 c.	Kidney Beans 3.5 c.	Chicken Breast 1.3 c.	Roast Beef 1.3 c.	Cheddar Cheese 1.7 c.

(Nutrition Data 2012)

The chart clearly shows us that it is easy to meet and exceed our RDA of protein with animal products. If we can only eat 1.3 cups of meat each day, that's not much food, but with plant foods it is just the opposite. We need to eat lots of them to reach the RDA. In the United States getting enough protein is typically not a problem. It's overconsumption of protein that is the problem. According to a National Health and Nutrition Examination Survey from 2007-2008, the average person consumes nearly twice the recommended amount (or four times the obligatory loss amount). The average man consumes 102 grams, and the average woman consumes 71 grams (Live Strong 2012). For the typical person those extra grams of protein come from animal foods, not plant foods.

The above chart shows us it is virtually impossible to eat enough of most plant foods to exceed the RDA for protein. More importantly, if we take a combination of these plant foods, with meat sparingly, we can easily meet 56 grams of protein a day and still consume all the essential nutrients.

Rather than looking at specific foods, let's consider the protein concentration in general. This will give us a broader picture of the amount of protein in various kinds of foods. The following chart shows about how many cups of each food type are needed to yield 56 grams of protein.

AMOUNT OF FOOD THAT YIELDS 56 GRAMS OF PROTEIN (in cups)							
Food Group	Meat	Dairy	Nuts	Legumes	Grains	Vegetable	Fruits
Cups	1-2	1-7	2-4	2-4	9-11	20-90	40-180

We see that meat is the most concentrated source of protein, fruit is the least, and the others are in between. Notice that nuts and legumes are very good plant sources of protein.

If the average person consumes twice as much protein as recommended, the question arises as to how much is too much? That varies from person to person, and the ideal amount is debated in the literature, from 5% to 35% of calories (56 grams is about 10%). However, we know Jonathan was eating too much because it was giving him symptoms. All the protein he was eating caused his gout. He had exceeded his limit.

Protein is an acid ash food and excess acid in the body depletes valuable minerals. Muscle soreness and spasms, and loss of bone density may occur when potassium and calcium are robbed from the body to neutralize this excess acid, as we indicated in the previous chapter.

Many doctors, scientists, and researchers have identified excess protein as a major cause of chronic degenerative diseases. *"Arthritis, diabetes, emphysema, cancer, AIDS, and circulatory disorders... are the result of... the long-term efforts of the body to process excess protein... brought about by sustained protein consumption intensified by long-term insufficiencies of fruits and vegetables in the diet...Our diets should be made up mostly of vegetables and fruit with only small amounts of meat, poultry and fish"* (M. T. Morter 1987).

Dr. T. Colin Campbell authored a study that examined mortality rates, diets, and lifestyles of 6,500 people in 65 rural

Gary's Story

Gary was active and healthy and never gave his diet much thought. Then at age 60 he was struck down with rheumatoid arthritis. His joints swelled up and became extremely painful. He couldn't do up a button and for a time, couldn't even get a fork to his mouth so had to be fed. It was difficult for him to get up and down or walk because of the pain in his hips. He lost 30 pounds and became extremely thin and weak. Medication gave him some relief but he was afraid of the side effects.

Gary loved candy and meat. When he learned how his diet could be the cause he gave them up and started eating lots more fruits, vege-tables and fresh juices. He slowly improved and within a year had regained his weight and overcome most of his symptoms. He learned that if he wanted to stay healthy, he could only eat meat and sugar sparingly.

counties in China for 20 years. He concluded that people with a high consumption of animal-based foods were more likely to suffer chronic disease like heart disease, diabetes, and cancer while those who ate a plant-based diet were the least likely. He wrote, *"People who ate the most animal-based foods got the most chronic disease ... People who ate the most plant-based foods were the healthiest and tended to avoid chronic disease. These results could not be ignored"* (T Colin Campbell 2012).

The actual amount of protein we need to consume daily is the amount it takes to keep our "house" in good repair. By eating a variety of plant foods, we can easily do that. When we include meat sparingly, we are not nearly as likely to develop the illnesses and diseases associated with consuming greater amounts of protein.

THE PROBLEM OF EXCESS FAT

It is not just eating excess animal protein that can cause health issues. Meat also contains high quantities of cholesterol and fat. Fat is known to *"...play a role in cardiovascular disease and type 2 diabetes... obesity and cancer"* (Mayo Clinic 2012). This is not news to most people. We have been taught the value of a low fat diet for years. *"Scientific studies dating from the late 1940s showed a correlation between high-fat diets and high-cholesterol levels... By the 1960s, the low-fat diet began to be touted ... as good for the whole nation. After 1980, the low-fat approach became an overarching ideology, promoted by physicians, the federal government, the food industry, and the popular health media"* (Berge 2008).

Animal fat is specifically designed by nature to store calories. It is personalized food storage. In the chart on the following page we can see that nuts are the only plant food that has a high percentage of fat calories in relation to animal products, and that all plant foods have some fat.

There is no obligatory loss of fat like there is of protein that requires a certain number of grams of fat per day. In other words, we don't use up a certain amount of fat each day that needs to be replaced. The only nutritional requirements for fat are the omega-3 and omega-6 essential fatty acids. Since almost all foods have some fat, it is nearly impossible not to get at least a little bit of fat in one's diet. The greater concern is getting too much. *"The fat content of the average American diet is in the range of 37 to 40 percent of calories"* (The Cancer Project 2012). Many authorities believe that is too high and the cause of many health problems. Some, like Dr. Dean Ornish in his heart disease reversal program, keep calories from fat to less than 10% (Dean Ornish 1995).

% OF CALORIES FROM FAT IN VARIOUS FOOD TYPES							
Fruits	Starchy Veggies	Legumes	Non-Starchy Veggies	Grains	Meat	Dairy	Nuts
1-5	1-5	3-5	10-15	10-20	20-75	20-75	60-90

The fat we eat is stored as fat in our body, and too much fat is detrimental to our health. When we eat meat sparingly, we limit the amount of fat in our diet. One reason that is important is because almost all the fat we eat is stored in our body as fat. Fat takes very little energy to digest. *"It is added to your body fat with a loss of only about 3% of its calories in the process"* (Neal Barnard 1993). In other words, 97% of the calories we eat as fat are stored as fat in preparation for that time when food is not available. That time rarely comes in our day since food is so plentiful. *"Accounting for waste, the average American consumed 2,673 calories per day in 2008 – an increase of 23% from 1970. More than 73% of U.S. adults are overweight or obese... and nearly 20% of children age 6-19 are obese. Physical inactivity and obesity accounted for 407,000 premature deaths in 2005"* (Center for Sustainable Systems 2011). We continue to eat more and more high fat foods and pay the price with added weight and poorer health.

We must note that meat is not the only source of fat responsible for excess calories. Dairy products, fried foods, vegetable oils, and salad dressings also add a significant amount of fat calories to the average person's diet and waistline. Vegetable oils weigh in at nine calories per gram, like any fat. They offer essential fatty acids, some Vitamin E and maybe a little Vitamin K, but other than t hat, they are empty foods. They contain no protein, no carbohydrates, and no fiber and are essentially devoid of minerals or any other vitamins. A tablespoon of olive oil contains about 120 calories. That is the same number of calories you would find in eight corn chips, or fifteen black olives, or a cup of fr ozen corn, or a large apple, or three cups of tomatoes, or thirteen cups of spinach. Because oils are simply liquid fats, even if they are made from plants, they would seem to fit best under the Meat Sparingly category of the Word of Wisdom.

BENEFITS OF MEAT

Let's look at three sample meats and three sample dairy products on the following page to see what they offer. We are including dairy under the Meat Group because it most closely resembles meat. Its nutritional composition is such that we might think of it as diluted meat or liquid meat.

Barry's Story

When Barry implemented the do's of the Word of Wisdom he was 80 pounds overweight, diabetic, and had high blood pressure, and high cholesterol. He said, "*I look back on this lifestyle change as one of the most significant things I have ever done. The improvements have gone far beyond the reversal of the disease in my heart's arteries. So many everyday problems have vanished – high blood pressure, diabetes, high lipids, indigestion, obesity, kidney stones, etc. I no longer need cholesterol, blood pressure or diabetes medication. More important, this is a treatment that I can feel and see. I now have a new lease on life.*"

Excess protein and fat are problems, but that doesn't mean we shouldn't eat meat. All the calories in meat come from either fat or protein. The only carbohydrate found in animal products is lactose, which is found in milk, and provides necessary glucose that all newborns need for energy. When there is a need for concentrated calories, such as in times of growth, hunger, or cold, animal products can be very beneficial.

FUEL RATIOS IN MEAT AND DAIRY PRODUCTS			
FOOD	% Calories from Carbohydrates	% Calories from Fat	% Calories from Proteins
Meat Roast Beef	0	45	55
Chicken Breast	0	36	64
Halibut	0	19	81
Dairy 2% Milk	39	35	26
Cheddar Cheese	2	72	26
Yogurt	42	22	36

Now let's look below at the essential nutrient composition of animal products. You will remember that essential nutrients are not made by the body and must be in the food we eat.

ESSENTIAL NUTRIENTS IN MEAT AND DAIRY PRODUCTS							
FOOD	Amino Acids	Vitamins	Minerals	Fatty Acids	Fiber	Water	Phyto-nutrients
Perfect Score	9	13	10	2	Yes	%	Abundant
Meat Roast Beef	9	10	10	2	None	64	None
Chicken Breast	9	11	10	2	None	63	None
Halibut	9	9	8	2	None	72	None
Dairy 2% Milk	9	13	9	2	None	90	None
Cheddar Cheese	9	10	9	2	None	37	None
Yogurt	9	12	9	2	None	85	None

Meat and dairy products contain all the essential amino acids and fatty acids plus nearly all the essential vitamins and minerals. From that perspective, they are beneficial. However, they do not contain fiber or phytonutrients. Plant foods must be eaten to obtain these essential nutrients.

The most beneficial reason to eat animal products for most people is Vitamin B12. It is the one essential nutrient found in animal products that is not found in plant foods. *"Vitamin B12 is found in foods that come from animals, including fish and shellfish, meat (especially liver), poultry, eggs, milk, and milk products... A deficiency can potentially cause severe and irreversible damage... to the brain and nervous system"* (Wikipedia 2012).

Although Vitamin B12 is found in animal foods it is not synthesized by plants or animals. Only bacteria make biologically active vitamin B12. When an animal eats food that contains these bacteria, it gets vitamin B12 into its system. When we eat that animal, we get the vitamin into our own system.

The RDA for Vitamin B12 is a tiny amount of six micrograms. This vitamin can be stored in the body, mainly in the liver, and *"... most people have at least a three year reserve of this vital nutrient"* (John A. McDougall 2007). Therefore, it does not need to be consumed every day. A person who eats meat or dairy products, even occasionally, or sparingly, should maintain adequate reserves of Vitamin B12.

IN TIMES OF WINTER, COLD, OR FAMINE

The counsel to eat meat sparingly makes it obvious that the Word of Wisdom is not a system of vegetarianism. That directive is reinforced in another revelation that says, *"And whoso forbiddeth to (eat meat)... is not ordained of God"* (D&C 49:18). Nevertheless, the Lord also counsels, *"And it is pleasing unto me that they (flesh of beasts and of the fowls of the air) should not be used, only in times of winter, or of cold, or famine"* (D&C 89:13). "Pleasing" the Lord is another compelling reason to consider how much meat we consume.

President Heber J. Grant credited his good health in old age to living the Word of Wisdom, emphasizing the limited use of meat. He said in a 1937 general conference address, at the age of 81, *"I think that another reason why I have very splendid strength for an old man is that during the years we have had a cafeteria in the Utah Hotel, I have not, with the exception of not more than a dozen times, ordered meat of any kind... I have endeavored to live the Word of Wisdom and that, in my opinion, is one reason for my good health"* (Grant 1937). President Grant's emphasis on his limited use of meat of *"...not more than a dozen times"* is instructive.

One reason meat is good to eat *"only in times of winter, or of cold"* is because of the thermic effect which we talked about in Chapter 5. It takes 20% to 30% of the energy consumed to digest and assimilate protein which warms up the body. It's like revving an engine. The fat in the meat is a convenient package of concentrated calories that "adds fuel to the fire." Meat is also obviously good to eat in *"times of famine"* because it can be lifesaving.

Protein is typically not burned as fuel. The body mainly uses glucose (from carbohydrates) and fat for fuel with glucose as the primary source. However, if the conditions are right, the body can burn protein for fuel as well. Therefore, another reason meat is good when starving is because protein is an important backup fuel source in addition to the fat in the meat.

Technically, protein is not burned for fuel. It is converted into glucose, and then the glucose is burned for fuel. This is a lifesaving and "expensive" process. It is lifesaving because it allows the body to use animal products as fuel when there is little else to eat. It is "expensive" because it costs a lot of *calories* to turn protein into glucose. For every two calories of protein eaten, about one calorie of glucose is produced (Bailor 2012). It takes a lot of energy to make that glucose molecule. Some of that energy is provided from the fat stores of the body, so a person loses weight.

"WINTER" WEIGHT LOSS PROGRAM

You may recognize the process I just described as a high protein / low carbohydrate weight loss diet. There are many of them out there, and maybe you have tried them. They mimic "times of winter or of cold or of famine" by restricting carbohydrates – fruits, vegetables and grains – and eating large amounts of protein and fat. These diets are good for weight loss because the more protein you eat, the more energy you expend converting the protein to glucose to be used as fuel. You spend more calories digesting the food than you get from the food. You become a "fat burning machine." The additional calories needed come from stored fat you have on your body, so you lose weight. It's like making a deal with your friend that every time you give him $2.00 he gives you $1.00 back. The more you do it the less money you have, so if your goal is to have less money, then it is a great program.

Though this "winter" weight loss program is effective, it should be remembered that the primary purpose of meat is to help us through lean and cold times. Meat supplies fuel to a backup system that is meant to be temporary. Essential fiber and phytonutrients are lacking in this program, and nutritional deficiencies and health problems may eventually arise from excess protein and excess fat as we have talked about. A much healthier and just as effective weight loss program is to follow the Word of Wisdom as it is written: keeping the don'ts and doing the do's.

> ### The Word of Wisdom Weight Loss Program
> Gayle gave up refined carbohydrates, like white bread, spaghetti, and cereals and switched her diet to lots of whole plant foods. She also cut way back on dairy products and meat and only consumed them occasionally. Though she didn't count calories or watch her food portions she still lost 30 pounds in two months.
> Janelle did the same thing as Gayle, in addition to walking 5 miles a day. Included in her diet were large amounts of green beans and potatoes, up to 5 baked potatoes a day. In six months she lost 100 pounds.

DAIRY PRODUCTS

We have included milk and other dairy products in the Meat Food Group as its nutritional content is very similar to meat that is diluted with water. Most people growing up in a Western or European culture have been taught that consuming milk is a necessary part of good health. In fact, Dairy is one of the five food groups in the U.S. and the United States Department of Agriculture (USDA) says we *need* three cups of milk a day (USDA 2012). After all, *"you need to drink your milk."*

Although milk has many important nutrients in it, there are two major reasons why it is not a *necessary* part of our diet, but rather it's optional.

1. **The majority of the people in the world cannot or do not drink cow's or goat's milk**. - Milk has a carbohydrate in it called *lactose*. Lactose is broken down during digestion by the enzyme *lactase*. *"At birth, all mammals produce the lactase enzyme and can therefore drink their mother's milk without experiencing bloating ,cramping or diarrhea. After weaning however, mammal infants stop producing lactase and prepare for an adult diet of raw meats, grass or other delicacies"* (Decode Me 2012).

   Humans are the same except for those who are descendants of generations of milk drinkers, such as in Europe or West Africa. In that case, lactase continues to be produced into adulthood, because of genetic adaptation. But the majority of people are intolerant to lactose after being weaned. *"Lactose intolerance ranges in frequency from 2-5% in Northern Europe and up to nearly 100% in Asia, South-Africa and Latin-America, with intermediate rates in North-America and North-Africa. An estimated 30 to 50 million American adults are thought to be lactose intolerant"* (Decode Me 2012). Those who are lactose intolerant may experience symptoms like diarrhea, nausea, abdominal cramps, bloating, and gas when they consume milk and other dairy products.

   It is also important to realize that much of the world's population thinks that drinking milk from another species is very strange. *"The aversion to milk drinking in China is particularly strong. Many Chinese find the notion of drinking a glass of milk absolutely revolting"* (Sherman 2002).

2. The "essential" nutrients in milk can also be obtained from plant foods. – Milk is often promoted as being necessary because of the essential nutrients it contains. We should remember that the only nutrient in milk that is not in plant foods is Vitamin B12. For that reason, we might want to consume some dairy products or meat occasionally, but all the other essential nutrients – amino acids, vitamins, minerals and fatty acids – are readily found in plant foods. After all, milk is made by cows eating only plant foods in the first place.

Another reason some individuals may want to be cautious about dairy products is that milk is the most common food allergen. It affects 65% of people with food allergies. Some of the most common complaints include "… *sinusitis, heartburn/reflux, constipation, diarrhea, irritable bowel syndrome, acne, arthritis, headaches, and ADHD"* (Wangen 2012). *"Cow's milk consumption is one of the most significant contributors to middle ear problems in children"* (Schmidt 2004). One way to test if symptoms are a result of milk is to eliminate all dairy products for two weeks. Typically an improvement will happen in that period of time if milk is the cause.

Although we are told we *need* milk, the Word of Wisdom does not mention it. If it was a necessary food, it would seem the Lord would have revealed it to the prophet Joseph along with herbs, fruits, meats, and grains. Instead, milk seems to fit best under the category of Meat

Emma's Experience
Dottie's three year old daughter, Emma, was *"drowning in mucous"*. She had been tested for allergies and was found allergic to all 85 things for which she was tested. Emma's favorite foods were cheese, milk, yogurt and ice cream. With a great deal of effort Dottie was able to cut way back on the amount of dairy products in Emma's diet. Along with that the allergies and mucous congestion disappeared.

Sparingly. To eat meat sparingly in times of winter, cold, or famine is a remarkable revelation. It was way ahead of its time when given, and in the current environment of nutritional science, it still is. Undoubtedly, health blessings come to those who follow it.

SCRIPTURAL INSIGHTS

In the Old Testament we read the story of Daniel and how he trusted in the Word of Wisdom of his day. He and his three friends had been taken captive by King Nebuchadnezzar. They were to be carefully nourished for three years, at which time they would stand before and serve the king. They were to eat the choicest of the king's food and wine to prepare them for that service, but because of their "Word of Wisdom" they refused to do so (Dan. 1:8).

The servant of the king argued that the king had made him responsible for training these young men and had commanded they should eat and drink the same as the others. If they did not, the king would see that they were growing weak and thin and would surely have the servant killed.

Daniel asked that he and his friends be allowed to follow the health habits that had been given to them. His request was that for ten days they would feed upon pulse (foods made of seeds, grains, etc.) and drink water to see if they were not healthier than all the rest. After ten days they looked better and appeared healthier than all the others, so they were allowed to continue. Although the king's wine and meat were undoubtedly considered the best foods available and believed to produce the highest level of health, Daniel and his friends had a higher law. Although their "diet" was not the popular one, it proved to be the best one.

In our day it is easy for most of us to eat like kings because food is plentiful, and choices are unlimited. Elder Joseph F. Merrell said, *"Americans eat too much meat... all the proteins needed are available in... other foods"* (Merrill 1978). It takes a lot of self-control to pass on meat and other tasty foods, but there is wisdom in doing so.

Elder LeGrande Richards also taught about eating meat sparingly, *"The Lord admonishes us to eat meat sparingly, an admonition that is also verified by the findings of science today,* *since an excess of meat can contribute to cardiovascular diseases. However, he didn't say that man should abstain totally from eating meat... The key is found in the word "sparingly"* (Richards 1950). President George Albert Smith, who succeeded President Grant as president of the Church, saw the need to eat meat sparingly too. His son-in-law recorded, *"President Smith's meals are simple and nourishing. In the summer he eats no meat, and even in the winter months he eats very little"* (Stewart 1950). Several of our Church leaders have considered the counsel to eat meat sparingly an important "do" of the Word of Wisdom.

The don'ts of the Word of Wisdom have been proven scientifically and are nearly universally accepted. The do's of the Word of Wisdom have also been proven, but their acceptance is not nearly as universal. There is still much debate in the scientific circles about what constitutes a good and healthy diet. Thankfully, we have the Word of Wisdom to point us in the right direction so we can receive the promised blessings of health.

Elder John A. Widstoe taught in General Conference of another benefit that comes from doing the do's, *"Perhaps, were we more careful to obey the part of the Word of Wisdom that deals with the 'do's' it might be easier to obey the 'don'ts,' and thereby be able more easily to conquer our appetites for the forbidden things. The more completely the body is able to function as intended by nature, the better control man has over himself and less desire he has for stimulants and for all things injurious"* (Widstoe 1926). This is a profound and true insight and of great practical worth to those who struggle with addictions.

SUMMARY: VARIABLE D – DOING THE DO'S – MEAT SPARINGLY

We have seen that animal products have an important, but limited role in our diet. In excess they can be detrimental to our health. The counsel to eat meat sparingly is a significant *do* in the Word of Wisdom, and when combined with Herbs and Fruits, brings us blessings of temporal and spiritual health:

1. **Food Group 1 – Herbs** – Eat lots of vegetables and legumes.
2. **Food Group 2 – Fruit** – Eat lots of fruit and some nuts.
3. **Food Group 3 – Meat Sparingly** – Eat sparingly of meats and dairy.

THE WORD OF WISDOM FORMULA			
KEEP THE DON'TS	+ DO THE DO'S	+ OBEDIENCE TO COMMANDMENTS	= PROMISED BLESSINGS

7

The 4 Food Groups – Grains

The more the don'ts and do the do's of the Word of Wisdom are kept, the more likely it is that health will improve and that symptoms will go away. When harmful substances are limited and nutritional quality is improved, the body is better able to function as it was designed. The following are a few examples of what frequently happens when a person more closely follows the don'ts and do's of the Word of Wisdom.

Roslyn and her husband had wanted a baby for four years, but she had been unable to conceive. They changed their diet, and within two months, Roslyn was pregnant. They had a healthy little daughter, and a couple of years later, daughter number two joined the family.

Richard had chronic heart burn. Changing his diet made it so he no longer needed his antacid medications. Trisha cured herself of chronic kidney infections, constant neck and lower back pain, and painful menstrual cycles. Donna saw a significant improvement in the anxiety and depression she dealt with frequently. Jan lost 90 pounds. Terri's night sweats and hot flashes significantly improved. Duane was no longer exhausted all the time and even felt like going to work in the mornings. Gerald's migraines of 25 years disappeared. Thane's 12 year bout with psoriasis went away. Suzanne no longer had seasonal allergies. Jack's sleep apnea improved, and he no longer needed oxygen at night. Don's arthritic pain faded, and the strength in his hands returned. Sharon's three year old son no longer had recurring ear infections. Sarah had type 2 diabetes and was able to discontinue insulin injections.

The main changes each of the above people had to make were in the do's. They ate significantly more foods from the first two Food Groups of the Word of Wisdom – Herbs and Fruit. They ate more sparingly from the third Food Group – Meat. They were also wiser in their food choices from Food Group 4 – Grain.

FOOD GROUP 4 – GRAIN

"All grain is ordained for the use of man... to be the staff of life... all grain is good for the food of man... nevertheless, wheat for man... barley... for mild drinks, as also other grain" (D&C 89:14, 16-17).

THE STAFF OF LIFE

The primary foods of life are grains. Historically they make up five out of the six staple foods eaten to sustain life and the world's population. *"Throughout civilization and around the world, six foods have provided our primary fuel: barley, maize (corn), millet, potatoes, rice, and wheat"* (John McDougall 2012). They are concentrated carbohydrates that provide a significant amount of energy for fuel and plenty of protein for normal building and repair of the body as seen in the sample grains below.

FUEL RATIOS IN GRAINS			
FOOD	% Calories from Carbohydrates	% Calories from Fat	% Calories from Proteins
Grains — Wheat	83	5	12
Grains — Rice	86	7	7
Grains — Oats	70	15	15

One of the remarkable advantages of grains is how well they store. If kept dry, they can be stored through hot and cold weather for decades. They don't have a season in which they must be eaten or preserved before spoiling like fruits and vegetables, so they are a food that can be depended on year round. They are like a *staff* that a person can lean on and trust and be supported by. Thus, they are the *staff of life*. Grains in their whole form, like other plants foods, have nearly all the essential nutrients. The few vitamins or minerals they may lack are easily made up by eating other whole, minimally processed foods.

ESSENTIAL NUTRIENTS IN GRAINS							
FOOD	Amino Acids	Vitamins	Minerals	Fatty Acids	Fiber	Water	Phyto-nutrients
Perfect Score	9	13	10	2	Yes	%	Abundant
Grains — Wheat	9	10	9	2	Yes	9	Abundant
Grains — Rice	9	9	9	2	Yes	10	Abundant
Grains — Oats	9	9	9	2	Yes	8	Abundant

(WHOLE) WHEAT FOR MAN

Although all grains are good, the Word of Wisdom singles wheat out as being especially useful for man. As a whole food, wheat is an excellent nutritional product. It can be used in its natural form as wheat kernels or wheat berries. *"President George Albert Smith ate boiled wheat, preferring whole wheat rather than cracked. He ate it like a cereal..."* (Allen 1998). Wheat can also be added to soups and salads. It can even be soaked, run through a meat grinder, and then used in many recipes as a replacement for ground meat.

Church members have long been admonished to have wheat in their food storage. President Ezra Taft Benson taught, *"Dry, whole, hard grains, when stored properly, can last indefinitely, and their nutritional value can be enhanced through sprouting, if desired"* (E. T. Benson 1974). Sprouting wheat, or any grain for that matter, increases its nutrients, *"...including B vitamins, vitamin C, folate, fiber, and essential amino acids.... Sprouted grains may also be less allergenic to those with grain protein (gluten) sensitivities"* (Whole Grains Council 2012). The nutritional quality of sprouted wheat is so good that a person could live on it and water indefinitely.

The more common use of wheat is flour. The nutritional composition of whole wheat flour is fairly similar to the wheat berry. Not much is lost in the milling process. However white flour is significantly different than the wheat from which it is ground. *"There is an average loss of 70-80% (of most nutrients) in refined and enriched flour"* (Ecological Agricultural Projects 1991).

Elder John A. Widstoe taught that wheat is best when used in its whole form or as whole wheat flour. He said, *"There is no reason for assuming that the Lord meant a part of the grain kernel (be used). The regular use of whole wheat bread and cereal would greatly increase our health and protect us against disease"* (Widstoe 1945).

The lack of nutrients in white flour make it a so-called "empty calorie" food. When eaten, white flour still provides

---

Amber's Story

"My grandmother died of a heart attack at age 30. My mother had a hysterectomy at age 30, was a diabetic on insulin shots, had high blood pressure and 5 heart attacks and died at age 65. Two of my brothers and one sister have enlarged hearts, high blood pressure and are diabetic. Both of my sisters had hysterectomies by age 30. My mother's siblings were all diabetic and her sisters all had hysterectomies by the time they were 30. We were all told we needed to be checked for these 'hereditary' conditions.

"I am 55 years old. I do not have high blood pressure, heart disease, an enlarged heart, diabetes or female problems. I still have my uterus. I take no medication. I have lived the do's and don'ts of the Word of Wisdom for the past 30 years and I know that has made the difference."

starch for energy, but the vitamins, minerals, and other nutrients that should accompany that starch have largely been eliminated. *"Because these refined grains lack the fiber and nutrient density... they also cause obesity, diabetes, heart disease, and significantly increased cancer risk"* (Joel Fuhrman 2003). Although there is much disagreement in nutritional science, most all authorities agree that white flour is a detriment to good health and a source of disease.

GLUTEN INTOLERANCE

One concern some people have about wheat is that they are allergic or sensitive to it. Some people react to gluten, which is the protein in wheat, barley, and rye, and may be diagnosed with Gluten Intolerance Syndrome or Celiac Disease. Others may not be diagnosed but still find they are sensitive to gluten and feel better when they avoid it. Digestive problems, fatigue, headaches, skin conditions, and even anemia are all common symptoms. It is becoming much more common *"...having increased fourfold in the last 50 years"* (Davis 2011).

Since the Word of Wisdom teaches "wheat for man," we might wonder why so many people seem to have an adverse reaction to it. There are at least five possible reasons. Let's look at these and what a person might do so he can eat wheat without reacting.

1. **Grains are acid ash foods** – When the protein in wheat is digested, an acid ash is the by-product. We talked about this with meat too. *"Grains such as wheat account for 38% of the average American's acid load, more than enough to tip the balance into the acid range"* (Davis 2011). Sometimes the adverse reactions to wheat are because a person is just eating too much acid ash food altogether. Such an individual needs to increase his fruits and vegetables and make his body more alkaline.

2. **Refined grains are worse than whole grains** – The lack of nutrients in white flour makes the body function less efficiently. Elder John A. Widstoe

warned of the adverse effects of processed foods, *"If the food is wholesome and sufficient, the body develops normally; if it is poor in quality or robbed of its vitality by being refined... the body will probably be stunted or diseased; or both" (Widstoe 1937).* Eliminating refined grain products from the diet and eating whole grains with all their nutrients instead may help eliminate gluten sensitivity for some people.

3. **Enzyme inhibitors** – Grains have phytic acid and enzyme inhibitors that keep them from sprouting, spoiling, or rotting. These allow grains to be stored in a dormant state for decades and are one reason grains are the staff of life. These protective chemicals can make digestion of grains much more difficult. *"Soaking allows enzymes, lactobacilli and other helpful organisms to break down and neutralize phytic acid... (and) also neutralizes enzyme inhibitors"* (Sally Fallon 1999). Soaking grains overnight, or even better, sprouting them neutralizes these chemicals and makes the digestion of wheat much easier.

4. **Short leavening times** – Yeast is put in dough to cause the dough to rise, but there is another purpose. The fermentation caused when the yeast reacts with sugar molecules helps break down and soften the gluten proteins making them easier to digest. It takes time for the gluten to break down. The more time the yeast ferments, the more the gluten is broken down, and the easier it is to digest. One author says, *"Fast-made bread is one of the most destructive implementations into the modern diet. It has become normal fare, and poorly-prepared and poorly-digested wheat is the chief contributor to the current plague of gluten-intolerance"* (Lawler 2008). Many people have found that baking their own bread using

a recipe that takes 12 to 24 hours makes the wheat gluten much more digestible.

5. **Wheat has changed** – The genetics of wheat are not what they used to be. The proteins in wheat have been altered by hybridization. *"It is not the same grain our forebears ground into their daily bread... it has changed dramatically in the past 50 years...Wheat glutens in particular undergo considerable structural change with hybridization. In one hybridization experiment, 14 new gluten proteins were identified in the offspring that were not present in either parent wheat plant* (Davis 2011). The ratio of starch to protein has been changed. These "new gluten proteins" may be hard for some people to digest. Old world wheat varieties, like emmer, einkorn, kamut and spelt are making a comeback because some people find they do not react to them like modern wheat.

THE WORD OF WISDOM SOLUTION

In Chapter 3 we quoted President Ezra Taft Benson speaking about the Word of Wisdom. That quote bears repeating here, *"...what need additional emphasis are the positive aspects--the need for vegetables, fruits, and grains, particularly wheat. In most cases, the closer these can be, when eaten, to their natural state-- without over-refinement and processing--the healthier we will be. To a significant degree, we are an overfed and undernourished nation digging an early grave with our teeth, and lacking the energy that could be ours because we overindulge in junk foods"* (E. T. Benson 1979).

White flour, white sugar, and all the refined and processed foods that go along with them are a major cause of poor health and disease. If we look at the food consumed in America, we can see quite easily how we are "digging an early grave with our teeth." The chart below shows the number of calories available per day per person from the US food supply. It is the amount of food that goes from the farm to the home, taking waste and spoilage into account.

CALORIES AVAILABLE PER DAY PER PERSON (Total = 2673 calories)							
Fruits	Veggies	Dairy	Added Sugars	Meat Eggs Nuts	Added Fats	Grains	Total
86	122	257	459	482	641	625	2673
3%	4.5%	9.5%	17%	18%	24%	23%	100%

You will notice there are seven groups of food in this chart: two of them, added sugars and added fats, are not listed in the Word of Wisdom. They represent "...*what the food industry uses to... make (food) more appealing in marketing to consumer.*" (Philpott 2011). Together, these two groups add up to an astonishing 1,100 calories – 41% of the total calories available! Remember these added foods are mainly "empty calories" containing very little, if any, of the essential nutrients the body needs to function properly.

Contrast that 41% of added sugars and fats to the total calories available from fruits, vegetables, and grains. There are 833 calories available in these three food groups, which *are* in the Word of Wisdom, or 31% of the total. Even in these three groups, much of the food eaten is highly processed. For example, five times more refined grains are consumed than whole grains (USDA 2005). The remaining 28% of calories comes from the dairy and meat groups, what most would consider not a "sparingly" amount.

As we consider these numbers, is it any wonder that health problems abound? How can we have health in the navel, marrow in the bones, run and not be weary, walk and not faint, and have the destroying angel pass us by, if we are not living the principle that brings these promised blessings to us?

Elder Widstoe defined the problem and the solution very well, "*It happens too often that those who have refrained all their lives from the things forbidden in the Word of Wisdom,* suffer from grave maladies, all too prevalent today. This must be in part, at least, the result of failure to obey the positive instructions of the Word of Wisdom, whether done willfully or ignorantly. Nature has no favorites; those who break any of the laws of health must suffer the consequences. Only when all the laws indicated in the Word of Wisdom are kept may one claim in full the promised reward that 'they shall receive health in their navel and marrow to their bone... and shall run and not be weary, and shall walk and not faint.' How many today may really claim these precious blessings? Conscientious study and application of this law of health, including its positive directions, will permit **all** to do so" (Widstoe 1937). This is a comforting and reassuring promise from Elder Widstoe. *All* who keep the don'ts and do the do's will received the promised blessings. It is our responsibility to learn what they are and then live them.

Greg's Story

"For 3 years I had tingly sensations and weakness that randomly moved between my arms, legs, neck and back. My chest would get tight and I would get trembles inside. Then I would get a sudden icky feeling and just feel awful. My head felt full and I had kind of a lump in my throat.

"I went to many doctors. I had my gall bladder removed, a brain scan, thyroid scan, several blood tests, treadmill test and several x-rays. I was told I had spurs in my neck, to lose weight, to take Motrin and to see a psychiatrist.

"Then I learned about how food could affect me. I changed my diet and now my symptoms are 90% better. I've learned that I have to watch what I eat!"

SUMMARY: VARIABLE D – DOING THE DO'S – GRAIN

Grain in its whole form is the staff of life. It lasts indefinitely and can be used in any season. When combined with the other three Food Groups, we receive promised the temporal and spiritual blessings of health the Lord has to offer us:

1. **Food Group 1 – Herbs** – Eat lots of vegetables and legumes.
2. **Food Group 2 – Fruit** – Eat lots of fruit and some nuts.
3. **Food Group 3 – Meat Sparingly** – Eat sparingly of meats and dairy.
4. **Food Group 4 – Grain** – Eat lots of whole grains.

THE WORD OF WISDOM FORMULA			
KEEP THE DON'TS	+ DO THE DO'S	+ OBEDIENCE TO COMMANDMENTS	= PROMISED BLESSINGS

Part 3

THE "O" VARIABLE
OBEDIENCE TO THE
COMMANDMENTS

8

WALKING IN OBEDIENCE TO THE COMMANDMENTS

In a recent Gospel Principles Sunday School class a lesson was taught on the Word of Wisdom. Testimonies surfaced as to how this revelation made a difference in people's lives, spiritually and with their health. Some spoke of experiences with things mentioned specifically in the Word of Wisdom, and others spoke of things they've learned are detrimental to their health.

The instructor talked about how he had fallen away from the church after his mission and had struggled with tobacco use for 25 years. He had successfully quit smoking six months earlier and had been able to return to the temple. He bore testimony of how he could not have done it without the Lord's help. He testified of how the spirit had come back into his life as promised in the Word of Wisdom and the difference the spirit had made.

Most of the participants in the class had something they wanted to say about the Word of Wisdom. Jane, who struggled with food addiction, added to the discussion she had learned that artificial sweeteners gave her intense stomach pains. Every three months for the past two years she'd had a medical procedure to cauterize chronic bleeding in her stomach. When she quit drinking soda pop with artificial sweeteners a few months earlier, the bleeding stopped. Now she no longer needed the procedure. Her husband added that he had been taking medication for many years due to a health condition caused by a former soft drink addiction. The brother next to him told how he had been addicted to Mountain Dew and had finally realized how bad it was when he noticed he had taken a can of pop out of the refrigerator and gulped it down before he even sat in his chair.

Then, Rachel chimed in with her story. She had confessed her Pepsi addiction to her bishop during a temple recommend interview. He replied that Pepsi wouldn't keep her out of the temple, and if she had a problem with it, that was her own personal Word of Wisdom issue. She soon gave up the pop, realizing that it was controlling her. Being controlled by a substance was contrary to the spirit and intent of the Word of Wisdom and was not what she wanted in her life.

Harold told the class that he had played guitar with a band for many years, and most of their gigs were in bars which subsequently led to an alcohol problem for him. He had since given it up and returned to activity in the Church. He testified of how blessed his life was now that he lived the Word of Wisdom.

Jacob said he had struggled with bowel problems since he was a teenager and he'd had 13 abdominal surgeries. Cutting way back on meat and eating lots of plant foods made a big difference in his digestion and he had gained significantly more strength. His health was the best it had been in 15 years.

Even though it was his first time attending and he was the only non-member in the class, Charles was willing to add to the discussion. An addiction to prescription drugs had cost him everything he owned and resulted in him living in the streets for a year. He had overcome that addiction five years earlier and was now re-married and holding down a good job. He said that now he was addicted to smoking and chewing tobacco and loved his beer but was trying to do better. He laughingly added that his wife was rationing his beer to two a night instead of five or six. He was happy to learn that the Stake had an addiction recovery class, and he committed to attend.

All these participants wanted to testify how keeping the don'ts, doing the do's, and walking in obedience to the commandments had blessed them with better physical health and an improved spiritual relationship with Heavenly Father. Although some confessed they still had lots of room for improvement, they all had a great appreciation for the Lord's Law of Health and its promises.

PHYSICAL EFFECTS OF SIN

President Spencer W. Kimball taught the importance of the promises in the Word of Wisdom and the foundation on which they are received. He said, *"In 1833 the Lord made promises which we should never take lightly: He said, '... the destroying angel shall pass by them ... and not slay them,' bringing back to our memory the days of Egypt. They shall have good health, he said, and strength and power with marrow in their bones and health in their navel. And perhaps even greater promises than those: 'And shall find wisdom and great treasures of knowledge, even hidden treasures' (See D&C 89:18–21). All these blessings to all of us who remember the sayings and walk in obedience"* (Kimball 1974). According to President Kimball there are two conditions on which we receive the promised blessings of protection, health, wisdom, and knowledge.

1. **Remember the sayings (to keep the don'ts and do the do's)**
2. **Walk in obedience (to the commandments)**

So far we have talked about how to "remember the sayings", keeping the don'ts and doing the do's, but doing that alone may not bring the desired blessings of good physical and mental health. We also need to walk in obedience to the commandments. In fact, many times that is the more important part.

Megan wasn't sleeping well at night and was cold and tired all the time. She had constant pain in her neck and upper back, frequent headaches, and a knot in her stomach. She changed her diet to eat more fruits, vegetables, and whole grain products, and eliminated soda pop, but her symptoms remained the same. She was frustrated that keeping the don'ts and doing the do's hadn't changed anything, but deep down inside, Megan knew what was wrong. She knew there was something else she needed to fix.

Megan had been married for three years, but it hadn't been easy. She and her husband had struggled to get along and had even been separated for a time. A few months earlier an old boyfriend began texting her. It was innocent enough the first few times, but Megan knew it was now out of hand. She was constantly afraid her husband would find out, and she knew it was her guilt and fear that was making her sick.

Megan finally resolved to fix her situation. She truly wanted her marriage to work ,so she ended her communication with her old boyfriend and blocked his number on her phone. Almost immediately her symptoms began to improve.

Megan's symptoms were caused by *not* walking in obedience to the commandments. She was living with the guilt of not being true to her marriage and the fear of her husband finding out.

President Ezra Taft Benson tells how sin can impact us physically, "*Sin debilitates; it affects not only the soul but the body... un-repented sin can diffuse energy and lead to both mental and physical sickness. Disease, fevers, and unexpected deaths are some of the things that have been directly related to disobedience*" (E. T. Benson 1979).

Megan's symptoms changed when she repented of the thing she was doing that was not in accordance with the commandments. The promised blessings, including blessings of health, could only come when she was walking in obedience.

PHYSICAL EFFECTS OF STRESS

Mental and physical sickness can be brought on by sin, but they can also be brought on by the stresses of life.

Kirk was afraid of having a heart attack. His heart seemed to flutter and skip beats. The first time it happened was when he was hiking on a P-Day on his mission. It scared him enough to go to the emergency room at the local hospital. Tests concluded nothing was wrong with his heart, but in the back of his mind, he always wondered.

The second episode came many years later when his wife had a seizure. He had to call for an ambulance to take her to the hospital. It was a very frightening and unnerving experience for him. His heart began to flutter and race, and he also ended up in the doctor's office. Tests once again concluded there was nothing wrong with his heart. From that point on, he frequently felt the arrhythmias and checked himself into the emergency room several more times when he became especially concerned. He was often searching on the internet for further explanation of his symptoms and talking to others about his problem, yet he couldn't get the fear of a major heart attack out of his mind. He went to several more doctors, including cardiologists, who all confirmed that he had no heart disease and that his symptoms were stress induced.

Kirk lived in fear. It made sense to him that stress was contributing to the heart palpitations, but he didn't know how to fix it.

There can be many causes of stress in a person's life. If stress is not handled appropriately, physical symptoms may begin to show up. Elder Joseph B. Wirthlin observed reactions caused by one of mankind's main stressors – money, *"The stress that comes from worry over money has burdened families, caused sickness, depression, and even premature death"* (Wirthlin 2004).

Newspaper headlines frequently report stress's link to illness. Headlines like these are common (Nano SRT 2012):

- Study Unravels Link Between Stress and Chronic Illness
- Reducing Stress May Improve Overall Heart Health, Study Finds
- Stress Can Make Allergies Worse
- Why Stress Kills – Study Shows How Stress Causes Illness
- How Stress Harms Your Physical and Psychological Health
- Irritable Colon Syndrome May be Caused by Food or Stress
- Psychological Stress and Susceptibility to the Common Cold
- Study Connects Workplace Turmoil, Stress and Obesity

SIN AND STRESS

Both sin and stress can create physical symptoms. Elder Richard G. Scott described these two causes of adversity this way, *"Trials, disappointments, sadness, and heartache come to us from two basically different sources.* **Those who transgress the laws of God** *will always have those challenges. The other reason for adversity is to accomplish the Lord's own purposes in our life that we may receive* **the refinement that comes from testing**. *It is vitally important for each of us to identify from which of these two sources come our trials and challenges, for the corrective action is very different"* (Scott 1995). In the next chapter, Chapter 9, we will talk about the physical effects of transgression and sin, how and why it manifests in the body, and what to do about it. In Chapter 10 we will do the same with the physical effects of stress, or *"testing,"* as Elder Scott calls it.

The emotional reactions to our experiences in life can make us physically, mentally, emotionally, and spiritually sick, but if we walk in obedience to the commandments, we create an internal environment that allows our bodies to heal and be well. How and why this works and what to do about it is the subject of "Part 3".

We need to reiterate what was said at the beginning of this book – walking in obedience to the commandments means *all* the commandments (Tanner 1972). You can't be selective and still expect to receive all the blessings.

There is one caution to note here. In situations that are potentially life threatening, like the previous story about Kirk, it is important to visit with your health care provider. You need to be checked out for any underlying medical issues. Applying the principles of the Word of Wisdom, in addition to any medical or health care treatment you may need, can only augment your health and well-being.

Applying the principles of these next two chapters will help you overcome both short-term and long-standing health problems. By adding "walking in obedience to the commandments" to your lists of don't and do's, you will discover what is often missing in your efforts to "run and not be weary, to walk and not faint, and to receive knowledge, even hidden treasures of knowledge." You will truly be able to comprehend and receive the blessings promised in the Lord's Law of Health.

SUMMARY: VARIABLE O – OBEDIENCE TO THE COMMANDMENTS

The third variable in the Word of Wisdom Formula is *Walking in Obedience to the Commandments*. In order to receive the promised temporal and spiritual blessings we need to:

1. Obey all the Commandments

THE WORD OF WISDOM FORMULA			
KEEP THE DON'TS +	DO THE DO'S +	OBEDIENCE TO COMMANDMENTS =	PROMISED BLESSINGS

9

SIN AND HEALTH

Jeremy suffered for years with depression, anxiety, digestive problems, insomnia, and chronic pain in his back, shoulders, and neck. At times he had been suicidal, and he was now taking several medications to help control his emotions and physical symptoms. He began cutting himself, but he abhorred himself for doing it. Even though he had tried many times to improve himself and get his life back on track, he had failed so often that he felt there wasn't any hope left for himself.

Jeremy had a remarkable, dream when he was a teenager that taught him how much the Savior loved and cared for him. It was still a vivid memory, 20 years later, yet it only magnified the stark contrast between what he felt the Lord expected of him and his real life of drugs, alcohol, and illicit sex. Jeremy was extremely frustrated and disappointed with himself. He couldn't comprehend how he could ever be well.

THE PHYSICAL MANIFESTATION OF SIN

The guilt and shame Jeremy was feeling for his many sins was a major source of his depression, pain, and other symptoms. Elder James E. Talmage tells us, *"In many instances... disease is the direct result of individual sin"* (Talmage 1915).

We see a parallel in the Book of Mormon with how Zeezrom's guilt made him deathly ill. Zeezrom had been a ring leader of those contending against Alma and Amulek. In Alma we read how he was opposed to that which was good:

Alma 10:31 And there was one among them whose name was Zeezrom. Now he was the foremost to accuse Amulek and Alma, he being one of the most expert among them...

Alma 11:21 ... Now Zeezrom was a man who was expert in the devices of the devil, that he might destroy that which was good; therefore, he said unto Amulek: Will ye answer the questions which I shall put unto you?

· Zeezrom asked his questions, but they backfired on him and he was confounded by the answers of Amulek and Alma. Humbled, he then wanted to know the truth.

Alma 12: 1, 7, 8 Now Alma, seeing that the words of Amulek had silenced Zeezrom, for he beheld that Amulek had caught him in his lying and deceiving to destroy him, and seeing that he began to tremble under a consciousness of his guilt, he (Alma) opened his mouth and began to speak unto him, and... Zeezrom began to tremble more exceedingly, for he was convinced more and more of the power of God... And Zeezrom began to inquire of them diligently, that he might know more concerning the kingdom of God.

Zeezrom's heart was converted, and he began to defend Alma and Amulek, but was cast out of the city because of his new-found beliefs. He then feared that Alma and Amulek had been put to death because of him. He felt extremely guilty that he had been the cause of their demise and was mentally suffering as a result. In Alma 15:3 we read,

*"And also Zeezrom lay sick at Sidom, with a burning fever, which was caused by the great tribulations of his mind on account of his wickedness, for he supposed that Alma and Amulek were no more; and he supposed that they had been slain because of his iniquity. And **this great sin, and his many other sins**, did harrow up his mind until it did become exceedingly sore, having no deliverance; therefore he began to be scorched with a burning heat."*

Zeezrom's burning fever was caused by the guilt he felt for his sins. Jeremy's guilt for his sins was causing depression, chronic pain, insomnia, and bowel troubles. How and why does guilt manifest itself in these ways? What is the connection between how we think and feel and how our bodies react? By knowing the answers to these questions, we can better understand why emotions affect us the way they do and how repentance and letting go can physically heal us.

THE AUTOMATIC BODY

There are three fundamental principles that help us understand how the body functions, and why sin and stress can manifest as physical and mental symptoms.

1. **The Body Works Automatically** – From the moment of conception, the body grows, develops, and functions without the need for conscious thought. Respiration, circulation, digestion, assimilation, and other processes run automatically. For example, the liver performs about five hundred functions, none of which are under conscious control. The heart beats and we breathe in and out without any conscious thought. We do all these things automatically without the need to think about how to do them.

2. **The Body is Designed to Survive** – The body is an instrument that responds to the needs of the moment. *"Everything your body does is directed to keeping you alive right now... this instant"* (M. Ted Morter 1995). For example, a person's heart rate is 70 beats per minute when sitting and increases to 150 beats per minute when running. The body makes that "survival" adjustment automatically in order to get more oxygen to the cells. Thousands upon thousands of physiological events take place constantly and simultaneously for the sole purpose of survival. Whenever a person eats, drinks, moves, or even thinks, his body immediately reacts accordingly. It is necessary in order to survive, and it is done automatically.

3. **Thoughts and Feelings Direct the Body** – The physical body receives thoughts and feelings as

directives from the mind and acts accordingly. A feeling of fear created by a honking horn when crossing a street causes one to jump. A desire to fast can override the natural desire to eat. Thoughts and feelings of sadness when a loved one passes away can cause tears. In all cases the body is simply doing what it is told by responding to the message it is receiving from the mind.

SURVIVAL REACTIONS

What would happen if the thought or feeling that "turns on" an action by the body is not "turned off," as if there was no end to the directive? With the examples above, a person would continue doing the action. He would continue to jump out of the way of the car, continue to fast and not eat, and continue to cry. Most of the time there is an end to the directive from the brain, so we don't have to worry about such unlikely results. However, what if the person doesn't move fast enough and actually gets hit by the car? How would he react the next time he heard a car horn honk? Or what if a person can't accept the loss of a loved one and never stops mourning? When would his tears stop? Such experiences can create a survival response that may never go away if not dealt with properly. As a result, a person may end up with chronic and even severe health conditions.

Steven had been in four car accidents and would get a migraine headache just by sitting in a car. Elena developed asthma after her young niece unexpectedly passed away. Tracy's blood sugar level skyrocketed and never returned to normal when her husband was arrested; soon afterward, she became a diabetic. Severe chest pains sent Alex to the emergency room ten different times, the first time being while he was going through a difficult divorce. Edward was making bread when he received news that his son was missing in action in the Viet Nam war; he could never eat wheat products after that without experiencing bloating and diarrhea. Kerry was unable to sleep at night and was afraid to go out in public. His problems started after he embezzled money from his employer, and even though he made amends, these problems persisted.

Whether it is a death in the family, a biting dog, speaking

in public, a car accident, or a myriad of other experiences, survival reactions are meant to be temporary. They are meant to get us away from the threat so we can be safe until that threat is resolved or goes away.

A survival reaction should be like turning a switch on and off, but it is often not that simple. The switch turns on when something stresses or threatens us, and should naturally turn off when it is over, so that our body returns to normal. A switch that stays on, for whatever reason, will eventually lead to some kind of physical or mental symptom.

Let's look closer at a few of our body's survival reactions and what may eventually happen if we don't turn the switch off and leave it on too long instead. Look at the chart on the following page. It shows the short and long-term reactions to stress:

> **Column 1 - Immediate Survival Reactions** – the body's normal, automatic reactions to a stressful situation.

> **Column 2 - Long-Term Survival Reactions** - symptoms that may occur if the "switch" does not get turned off and survival reactions continue. These reactions are necessary because of the thoughts and feelings associated with events, but are undesirable for good health if they persist.

> **Column 3 - Possible Chronic Conditions** – eventual chronic diseases and conditions that may be diagnosed when long-term survival reactions continue.

FEAR IS PRIMARY

If we analyze the thoughts and feelings that cause the physical reactions we don't like, we find they are all negative. Fear, anger, jealousy, revenge, greed, guilt, hate, worry, rejection, selfishness, and judgment are just a few of the emotions that will cause the reactions in the chart above. Of these feelings, fear is primary while all the others are secondary. It is the fear of what people think, the fear of failure, the fear of being wrong, the fear

BODY'S SURVIVAL REACTIONS			
SYSTEMS OF THE BODY	IMMEDIATE SURVIVAL REACTION	LONG-TERM REACTION (SWITCH STAYS ON)	POSSIBLE CHRONIC CONDITIONS
MUSCULAR	Tense and tight muscles and joints	Muscle pain and spasms, joint pain and inflammation, loss of muscle control	Fibromyalgia, cramps, tendonitis, arthritis, bursitis, MS, Parkinsons
CIRCULATION	Increased heart rate – to get more blood to body	Palpitations, arrhythmias	Anxiety, panic attacks, heart failure
	Elevated triglycerides and cholesterol – for energy production	High triglycerides and cholesterol	Heart disease
	Increased blood pressure – to get more blood to the body	High blood pressure	Heart disease, stroke
RESPIRATION	Increased – to get more oxygen to body	Shallow, rapid breathing	Dizziness, asthma
DIGESTION	Slows down – need to run or fight, not digest	Poor digestion, deficiency of acid and enzymes	Acid reflux, constipation, hiatal hernia
	Speeds up – need to evacuate bowels so can run or fight	Rapid digestion, excess acid, frequent bowel movements	Ulcers, diarrhea, IBS, Crohn's
HEALING	Slows down – need to run or fight, not heal	Weak immune system, injuries slow to heal	Colds, flu, cancer, autoimmune disease
HORMONES	Increased energy from thyroid and adrenals	Exhaustion – can't run or fight forever	Chronic fatigue, thyroid, adrenal failure
	Decreased reproductive – can't get pregnant	Hormonal imbalances, menstrual irregularities	Decreased sex drive, PMS, sterile, endometriosis
	Increased blood sugar – for energy	Elevated blood sugar levels	Diabetes
SLEEPING	No desire for sleep – need to fight	Inability to go to sleep or stay asleep though tired	Exhaustion, fatigue
	Sleep all the time – need to escape	Never can get enough sleep	Exhaustion, fatigue
MENTAL	Increased mental acuity – need to solve problem	Think too much, mind races, can't turn mind off	Anxiety, panic attacks, ADHD, bipolar
	Decreased mental acuity – need to escape	Depression, discouragement from no solution	Depression, bipolar, suicidal

of physical or emotional pain, etc. that is the major problem.

Fear, however, is not always bad; it does serve a purpose. Fear may keep us from walking too close to the edge of a cliff, grabbing something too hot, or making an unwise investment. It is, however, only meant to be temporary. Fear comes naturally to protect us from harm and enables us to survive. It is a vital component of our survival instinct. When we continue to hang on to fear, it will eventually cause this normal physical reaction to become an unwanted symptom or condition. Somehow, we need to be able to turn fear off.

HEALING FROM SIN

We can learn how to turn off negative emotions. Let's return to Zeezrom who now believed what Alma and Amulek had taught, yet he knew he had been a ringleader in blinding the people's minds against them. He tried to defend them but the people cast him out of the city. Alma and Amulek had been in prison *"many days"* (Alma 14:23) since Zeezrom had last seen them, and that whole time, he feared they were dead and believed that it was his fault! Zeezrom's "long-term reaction" to his guilty feelings was to be bed-ridden with a burning fever. *"And this great sin, and his many other sins did harrow up his mind until it did become exceedingly sore, **having no deliverance;** therefore he began to be scorched with a burning heat"* (Alma 15:3).

A mind "having no deliverance" will always yield physical or mental illness of some kind. The guilt and fearful thoughts that had "turned on" Zeezrom's physical reactions had not yet been "turned off," so suffering became inevitable.

When Alma and Amulek arrived at Zeezrom's bedside, he asked them to heal him. Alma's reply is very important. He said, *"Believest thou in the power of Christ unto salvation? ... If thou believest in the redemption of Christ thou canst be healed"* (Alma 15:6-8).

It is interesting to note that Alma did not ask Zeezrom if he had faith to be healed or even if he believed in the power of Christ to heal. Rather, he asked Zeezrom if he believed in the power of Christ unto salvation. In other words, he asked him if he believed in the atonement. Alma's question is powerful and insightful because Zeerom's "disease" was caused by feelings of guilt from sins and only the atonement of Christ can free a person from guilt. Zeezrom's subsequent healing miracle came as a result of his faith in the atonement of Christ, not his faith to be healed, a subtle but important difference.

The scripture story continues,

9 And (Zeezrom) said: Yea, I believe according to thy words.

10 And then Alma cried unto the Lord, saying: O Lord our God, have mercy on this man, and heal him according to his faith which is in Christ.

11 And when Alma had said these words, Zeezrom leaped upon his feet, and began to walk....

12 And Alma baptized Zeezrom unto the Lord; and he began from that time forth to preach unto the people.

In this story we see a pattern for healing from sin. It is the conversion pattern that members of the Church are familiar with. Zeezrom exercised faith, repented, was baptized, and immediately began serving the Lord. Because his mind was freed from guilt through the atonement, his body could function normally again. If we follow this pattern we can be healed from the physical effects of sin just like Zeezrom.

The survival "switch," that had been turned on when Zeezrom first recognized he had sinned, had finally been turned off in a very dramatic and immediate way. He "leaped upon his feet" to full recovery. Jeremy, who was mentioned at the beginning of the chapter, had already followed the same

Andreas's Experience

Andrea's neck, shoulder and arm pain started when she was running on the tread mill. She learned it was her thoughts and feelings that kept her from getting better. Andrea said, *"When my neck starts to stiffen up, I ask myself, 'What am I thinking about?' Each time I find I am irritated about something. They are different things, but I am always feeling irritated. I then can let it go and feel my neck and shoulder relax."*

four steps years earlier. He had exercised faith, repented, been baptized, and had served in the Church, but his health kept deteriorating. His survival switch was still turned on and he was having lots of physical and mental problems. Jeremy was missing something important.

3 STEPS TO ENDURING FAITH

In Moroni 6:4-8 we can discover the answer to why Jeremy was not healthy. Here, Moroni tells us there are three important steps a person must take to stay strong in the faith. After repenting and being baptized into the Church, Moroni says the new converts were "...*numbered among the people of the church of Christ; and their names were taken, that they might be remembered and* **nourished by the good word of God, to keep them in the right way, to keep them continually watchful unto prayer, relying alone upon the merits of Christ,** *who was the author and the finisher of their faith... as oft as they repented and sought forgiveness, with real intent, they were forgiven."*

The three steps are:

1. **Be Nourished by the Good Word of God** – An important resource for being nourished by the good word of God is the scriptures. President Henry B. Eyring taught, *"Throughout my life, the scriptures have been a way for God to reveal things to me that are personal and helpful... about my needs, my situation, and my life"* (Eyring 2005). Jeremy needed to diligently study his scriptures daily so he could learn what God would have him know and do.

2. **Be Continually Watchful unto Prayer** – Elder David A. Bednar said, *"We are commanded to pray always to the Father in the name of the Son. We are promised that if we pray sincerely for that which is right and good and in accordance with God's will, we can be blessed, protected, and directed"* (Bednar 2008). Jeremy needed to pray sincerely so he could be blessed, protected, and directed.

3. **Rely Alone upon the Merits of Christ** – Christ is the author and finisher of our faith. It starts with Him, continues with Him, and ends with Him. President Dieter F. Uchtdorf taught, *"Having faith in Jesus Christ and in His Atonement means relying completely on Him—trusting in His infinite power, intelligence, and love. When we have faith in Christ, we trust the Lord enough to follow His commandments—even when we do not completely understand the reasons for them. In seeking to become more like the Savior, we need to rely, through the path of true repentance, upon the merits of Jesus Christ and the blessings of His Atonement"* (Uchtdorf 2009). Jeremy needed to have faith in Christ, keep His commandments, and rely upon the atonement.

Jeremy weighed himself against all three steps and found he was falling short. He made little time for the essential daily, spiritual practices of scripture study and prayer. He didn't fully understand the power of the atonement of Jesus Christ, so he had a hard time relying on it. Even though he believed in Christ and had tried to repent many times, he didn't know how to make Christ's atonement an active part of his daily life in order to relieve his burdens and stay on the right path. He felt guilty for the pain he had caused Christ to suffer and felt he had disappointed Heavenly Father.

Many of us are very much like Jeremy. We fall short in doing the things we know we should, and we feel guilt or shame for it. We focus on our shortcomings rather than the solutions Heavenly Father has provided for us. This not only has spiritual implications, it can contribute to poor physical and mental health.

PRAYER AND SCRIPTURES

The solutions outlined by Moroni are scripture study, prayer, and continued trust in the atonement by repenting often and walking in obedience to the commandments. These solutions are so basic that we sometimes overlook or forget them, but they are the true source of healing from and overcoming sin. If health symptoms we have are the result of guilt or shame, then these solutions are not only spiritually essential for us, they are physically vital as well.

Elder Richard G. Scott told how reading the scriptures can benefit us emotionally and even help us heal physically. He said, *"Scriptures can calm an agitated soul, giving peace, hope, and a restoration of confidence in one's ability to overcome the challenges of life. They have potent power to heal emotional challenges when there is faith in the Savior. They can accelerate physical healing"* (Scott 2011). Gaining peace, hope, and confidence through the scriptures turns off the survival switch and physically, emotionally, and mentally we improve.

In the *For the Strength of Youth* pamphlet we are encouraged to ask ourselves this question, *"Am I living the way the Lord wants me to live?"* We are then counseled to implement the three steps, *"To help you become all that the Lord wants you to become,*

Shelly's Story
Shelly lived next door to her father-in-law, but as the result of a conflict, they had not spoken to each other for two years. She wanted to mend their relationship and thought about it often for six months, but before she could get up the nerve to talk to him, he had a heart attack and passed away. She felt horrible guilt for not having made amends with him before he died.

She went to her Heavenly Father in prayer and poured her heart out to Him. She talked to Him about her feelings, repented for her actions and attitude, and expressed gratitude for the atonement which fixed what she could no longer fix. Shelly had a wonderful healing experience. She felt at peace again, and her back pain, headaches, poor digestion, allergies, and insomnia of the past two years all dramatically improved.

1. Kneel each morning and night in prayer to your Father in Heaven...

2. Study the scriptures each day and apply what you read to your life...

117

> **3. Strive each day to be obedient... If you make a mistake, don't give up on yourself"** (The Church of Jesus Christ of Latter-day Saints 2011).

Once Jeremy understood the critical importance of these three steps, he committed to do them consistently. He did fairly well for a while but then would miss a day or two of reading his scriptures or saying his prayers. This was when he would slip and give in to temptation. The obvious difference in his ability to resist temptation when he was studying his scriptures daily and praying, and when he was not, became glaringly apparent. He learned how to apply what he read in the scriptures to his personal life, how to recognize answers to his prayers, and how to be more consistent. Jeremy's physical symptoms began to improve as he felt a closer relationship with the Lord and better about himself.

HEALING THROUGH THE ATONEMENT

It can take time to develop the daily habits of prayer and scripture study and to realize the importance of being consistent. These two steps are measureable, however, so we at least know if we have done them or not. What is often more difficult is learning to consistently rely upon the merits of Christ – to trust in the atonement and give up negative, fearful ways of thinking.

Jeremy felt guilty that he had sinned and made wrong choices that intensified Christ's suffering. He felt guilty that he disappointed Heavenly Father. Such feelings are not freeing and indicate that we do not understand the atonement. Sometimes we think if we can just be perfect and never make another mistake then, and only then, we will be good enough for the atonement. We quote "...it is by grace that we are saved, after all we can do" (2 Nephi 25:23). Since we know we can do more, we think we still fall short and aren't yet worthy of His grace.

Elder Ronald E. Poelman clarified, "(Some) are burdened by past mistakes, large and small, because of an incomplete or incorrect understanding of our Father's plan of redemption and mercy... One who assumes that he can or must pay the price for his sins and thereby earn divine forgiveness will not feel free to continue progress toward realizing his divine potential, that is, *eternal life. The fact is we cannot save ourselves"* (Poelman 1993). The atonement is a gift. It was offered out of love by our Savior, Jesus Christ. It covers all our sins individually, and it covers all of us collectively.

Elder Richard G. Scott additionally taught, *"Should choices be wrong, they can be rectified through repentance. When its conditions are fully met, the Atonement of Jesus Christ, our Savior, provides a release from the demands of justice for the errors made. It is wondrously simple and so incomparably beautiful"* (Scott 2012). Allowing the atonement to work in our lives is an essential part of healing.

Jeremy was grateful to relearn these concepts about the atonement, but he had another concern that was not unique to him. He questioned how he could ever be forgiven for the awful things he had done especially when he had done them repeatedly and he knew better. The General Authorities of the Church have given great counsel on how to do this. Elder Richard G. Scott shared this important insight, *"Satan would have you believe that serious transgression cannot be entirely overcome. The Savior gave His life so that the effects of **all** transgression can be put behind us, save the shedding of innocent blood and the denial of the Holy Ghost"* (Scott 2010).

President Dieter F. Uchtdorf made another important point. *"When the Lord requires that we forgive all men, that includes forgiving ourselves. Sometimes, of all the people in the world, the one who is the hardest to forgive—as well as perhaps the one who is most in need of our forgiveness—is the person looking back at us in the mirror"* (Uchtdorf 2012).

Self-forgiveness is indeed the most difficult part of the repentance process for most of us. We are not perfect and never will be in this lifetime. Elder Russell M. Nelson cautioned, *"When our imperfections appear, we can keep trying to correct them. We can be more forgiving of flaws in ourselves and among those we love"* (Nelson 1995). We are all sinners and have a great need for the redeeming gift of the atonement. Elder Neil L. Andersen said, *"For most, repenting is quiet and quite private, daily seeking the Lord's help to make needed changes"* (Andersen 2009). Repentance should be a gift that we use daily, and our partaking of the sacrament should be a weekly recommitment to become even more like the Savior. It's a continual process to be used for sins both big and small. For some, like Zeezrom, change through the atonement can be dramatic and immediate. For most of us, it is a constant striving to get closer to the Lord through our obedience, leaving the "natural man" behind. It's a constant daily effort but is just as effective and meaningful as Zeezrom's experience.

CHANGING BELIEFS

Repentance through the gift of the atonement is life-changing because we see and feel things differently. It can also be health-changing if the physical problems we have are tied to our beliefs.

It is important to understand that Zeezrom ended up in bed with a burning fever because of a change in beliefs. Had his beliefs not changed, he never would have felt guilty and never would have become so sick. Zeezrom had been a highly respected professional, "...*the foremost to accuse Amulek and Alma*" (Alma 10:31) and an "...*expert in the devices of the devil, that he might destroy that which was good*" (Alma 11:21). However, through Amulek's testimony the spirit was able to touch his heart and "...*Zeezrom began to tremble*" (Alma 11:46). When Alma added his testimony, "*Zeezrom began to tremble more exceedingly, for he was convinced more and more of the power of God*" (Alma 12:7).

As the power of God worked in him, Zeezrom's perspective changed, and he became seriously interested in Alma and Amulek's message. He "...*began to inquire of them diligently, that he might know more concerning the kingdom of God*" (Alma 12:8). As the truth settled in his mind, his beliefs were dramatically transformed. He realized that Alma and Amulek were speaking the truth and he was the one who was wrong. This 180 degree shift in belief caused him to be "*astonished at the words which had been spoken*" and recognize the damage he had caused "*among the people by his lying words; and his soul began to be harrowed up under a consciousness of his own guilt; yea, he began to be encircled about by the pains of hell*" (Alma 14:6). This change of belief that caused Zeezrom to see himself as a sinner, accompanied by his belief that Alma and

ע

Amulek were dead because of him, "... *did harrow up his mind until it did become exceedingly sore, having no deliverance; therefore he began to be scorched with a burning heat*" (Alma 15:3).

Our beliefs are powerful factors in causing our bodies to do what they do. Zeezrom's sins contributed to his fever because he now believed he was sinning. He felt guilty, and his body reacted to that guilt. He never would have had this particular fever if he had not come to that belief! Likewise, he never would have overcome the guilt and healed if he had not come to the belief that Christ paid for his sins. The guilt, however, was worth it because it allowed Zeezrom to repent and experience the "*... joy which none receiveth save it be the truly penitent and humble seeker of happiness*" (Alma 27:18).

We learn from Zeezrom that our body responds to our beliefs whether or not our beliefs are true. Zeezrom thought Alma and Amulek were dead on account of him, when in reality, they weren't. The additional guilt he felt for causing their supposed demise affected him just as much as if they really had died. His burning fever partly resulted from this false belief. His body wasn't reacting to what was actually true; it was reacting to what Zeezrom *believed* was true.

Heidi's Story

Heidi had a hard time sleeping, frequent vomiting for no apparent reason, migraines and a great deal of anxiety. She had made many poor choices in her life and was full of guilt, blame and regret. She couldn't forgive herself for the things she had done wrong.

Heidi had been raised in the Church and knew that Christ's atonement paid the price for sin. She just had a hard time believing that it paid for *her* sins. Through sincere prayer and fervent and daily scripture study she gained spiritual insights that allowed her to understand that she too was forgiven. With the relief of guilt came the relief of her physical ailments. The migraines and vomiting went away and the sleep and anxiety significantly improved.

The body doesn't discern the difference between what is true and false. That is the responsibility of the mind. The body just responds to how we think and feel. It is an instrument that responds like a hammer wielded in the hand of a carpenter. The mind that thinks and feels is the carpenter which tells the hammer what to do. The mind instructs the body and the body responds to the message. The body doesn't argue with the mind, and just does what it is told.

When Jeremy became more diligent and faithful in reading his scriptures and saying his prayers, he began to feel the effects of God's hand in his life. He recognized answers and direction and also found peace that he hadn't experienced in a long time. This peace and contentment sent a very different message to his body. His guilt, frustration, and discouragement were overpowered by the sweet peace of the spirit. As a result his back and neck pain began to dissipate, and he was able to sleep better at night. This improvement happened because his beliefs and perspective changed. Because he saw things differently, his body responded differently.

BENEFITS OF GUILT

Guilt can be a good thing for us. It was good for Zeezrom and Jeremy because it caused a change that was more in keeping with the will of God. Elder Boyd K. Packer taught that the *"...feeling of guilt is to the spirit what pain is to the physical body."* It tells us something is wrong and we need to do something about it. Elder Packer also added, *"We know that some anxiety and depression is caused by physical disorders, but much (perhaps most) of it is not pain of the body but of the spirit"* (Packer 2001).

Jeremy's anxiety, depression, suicidal thoughts, and cutting indicated that he was hurting spiritually and emotionally. Physical and emotional symptoms, like Jeremy's, can result from guilt. Guilt is inspired of the spirit and is meant to bring us to repentance. In both Zeezrom's and Jeremy's cases, guilt caused them to have a change of heart and repent.

It takes courage and humility to resolve guilt. It is not easy to apologize, make amends, or confess serious sins to the bishop, but if we do repent, we are freed and the guilt goes away.

Spiritually, emotionally, mentally, and physically we feel a whole lot better. *+ socially*

THE BURDEN OF SHAME

Another emotion that may accompany guilt, that also needs to be resolved, is shame. Elder Packer said, *"Too many of us needlessly carry burdens of guilt and shame"* (Packer 2001). Although these emotions are closely related, a useful distinction can be made. One researcher defined these terms this way, *"Shame is not guilt. Shame is a focus on self. Guilt is a focus on behavior. Shame is 'I am bad'. Guilt is 'I did something bad.'... 'I'm sorry. I made a mistake.' That is guilt. Shame is 'I'm sorry. I am a mistake!"* (Brown 2012). There is a huge difference between guilt and shame when defined in this manner. As we try to overcome guilt we apologize for DOING something wrong. This is inspired by the spirit and is freeing and powerful. Although it is difficult, we can try to make amends, summon the courage, and face the one we have wronged or talk to the bishop.

As we try to overcome shame we apologize for BEING something wrong. This is nearly impossible, for how can we change who and what we are? It is like trying to change one's height or eye color. This flawed belief can lead to addictive and defensive behaviors. *"Shame is highly, highly coordinated with addiction, depression, violence, aggression, bullying, suicide, and eating disorders"* (Brown 2012). Shame comes from listening to the lies of Satan. It is he who tells us we are of no worth. God tells us the opposite, that we are of *great* worth (D&C 18:10).

We must change our beliefs in order to heal from shame-caused symptoms and behaviors. *"I am of worth."* *"God loves me."* *"My actions may be wrong, but I still matter."* These are the beliefs we need in order to overcome shame and move on in a positive direction. President Dieter F. Uchtdorf counseled, *"At times we may even feel insignificant, invisible, alone, or forgotten. But always remember—you matter to Him!* (Uchtdorf 2011).

Jeremy's biggest hurdle in healing and overcoming his depression, anxiety, and self-destructive behaviors was in changing how he saw himself. *"There is something wrong with me!"* and *"I am so bad! How could God ever forgive me?"* were phrases he repeated often.

Jeremy said the thing that helped him heal the most was coming to believe he "mattered to God." He learned God loved him for who he was not for what he did. He said, *"I have learned that repentance is a process and that Heavenly Father knows that. He's not giving up on me if I don't get it right as quickly as I would like. He's never given up on me and he won't!"*

CRIPPLED BECAUSE OF SIN

There are two stories in the New Testament that are unique because they tell of men who were crippled as a result of sin. Christ healed them by forgiving them of their sins. Based on what we know about the effect of sin on the body, it is likely that their sins contributed to their physical ailments.

A man with palsy (a kind of paralysis) was taken to Jesus to be healed. Because there was no room in the house, his friends let him down on a cot through the roof. *"Jesus seeing their faith said unto the sick of the palsy; Son, be of good cheer; thy sins be forgiven thee"* (Matthew 9:2). The man was immediately healed, rose from his bed, and walked. Elder James E. Talmage commented on the connection between this man's palsy and sin, *"The man was probably in a state of fear; he may have known that his ailment was the result of wicked indulgences; nevertheless, though he may have considered the possibility of hearing only condemnation for his transgression, he had faith to be brought. In this man's condition* **there was plainly a close connection between his past sins and his present affliction"** (Talmage 1915, 179). Whatever his sins were, it appears they were literally weighing him down.

In the second story Christ healed a bed-ridden man at the pool of Bethesda who had an infirmity of 38 years. Later, Christ found him in the temple and said to him, *"Behold, thou art made whole: sin no more, lest a worse thing come unto thee"* (John 5:14).

Commenting on this healing, Elder Talmage said, *"**The man had probably brought about his affliction through his own sinful habits.** The Lord decided that he had suffered enough in body, and terminated his physical suffering with the subsequent* *admonition to sin no more"* (Talmage 1915).

Stories of Christ healing and changing lives of people in the New Testament are easy for most of us to believe. It's often more difficult to believe that Christ still has this power today and is just as willing to heal us now. He does have it, and He is willing! The healing power of God and His son Jesus Christ is available to us just as it was in the time of Christ's ministry on the earth. So how can we experience this freedom from sin and its consequences?

FREEDOM FROM SIN

If sin is contributing to our poor physical and mental health, we need to do the same things Jeremy did to get well. We need to use daily prayer and scripture study to guide us and also rely on the merits of Jesus Christ to save us from our sins and short-comings. We need to examine our beliefs and realign them when necessary. We need to repent and overcome guilt and shame.

Although these steps may seem difficult, none of us are beyond the reach of heavenly help. Elder Jeffrey R. Holland declared, "... *however late you think you are, however many chances you think you have missed, however many mistakes you feel you have made or talents you think you don't have, or however far from home and family and God you feel you have traveled, I testify that you have not traveled beyond the reach of divine love. It is not possible for you to sink lower than the infinite light of Christ's Atonement shines"* (Holland 2012). There is hope for all of us! God's love extends far beyond anything we may or may not have done. Following these steps and becoming free of sin is an important part of "walking in obedience to the commandments". Then we can have the promised blessings of health.

SUMMARY: VARIABLE O – OBEDIENCE TO THE COMMANDMENTS

The third variable in the Word of Wisdom Formula is *Walking in Obedience to the Commandments.* In order to receive the promised temporal and spiritual blessings we need to:

1. Obey all the Commandments by:
- Repenting and being free from sin.

THE WORD OF WISDOM FORMULA			
KEEP THE DON'TS	DO THE DO'S	OBEDIENCE TO COMMANDMENTS	PROMISED BLESSINGS

10

STRESS AND HEALTH

Joan had controlled her diabetes for many years through diet. When her blood sugars suddenly worsened, she had to go on insulin. About that same time, her thyroid began to fail, she was fatigued all the time, and was put on thyroid medication. She also began to have heart palpitations. A few times she'd even had anxiety attacks, so she started taking medication to control that. When Joan learned that stress could be the cause of such symptoms, she realized why her health had deteriorated. Her symptoms all began when her husband left the Church which had been an extremely stressful time for her.

This increased stress in Joan's life is the reason her blood sugar problems worsened and why she started having thyroid problems and anxiety attacks. She didn't know how to deal with her husband's choices so her survival switch had stayed "turned on."

THE PHYSICAL MANIFESTATION OF STRESS

In the previous chapter we discussed how unresolved sin can lead to physical ailments. Stress does the same thing, and for most of us, stress is a much more common cause of our symptoms than sin. Stress turns on the "switch" of survival reactions just like sin does, and if not turned off, it will lead to all kinds of physical and mental symptoms.

The chart of survival reactions on page 114 shows how the long-term reaction to stress can lead to diabetes, thyroid problems, and anxiety attacks. The segment of the chart that relates to these three conditions is below.

SYSTEMS OF THE BODY	IMMEDIATE SURVIVAL REACTION	LONG-TERM REACTION (SWITCH STAYS ON)	POSSIBLE CHRONIC CONDITIONS
HORMONES	Increased energy from thyroid and adrenals	Exhaustion – can't run or fight forever	Chronic fatigue, thyroid, adrenal failure
	Increased blood sugar – for energy	Elevated blood sugar levels	Diabetes
MENTAL	Increased mental acuity – need to solve problem	Think too much, mind races, can't turn mind off	Anxiety, panic attacks, ADHD, bipolar

When a person is stressed like Joan, the amount of sugar in the blood naturally increases. This additional sugar provides the energy necessary for her to run or fight, two ways of dealing with this "frightening" situation. This is part of what is known as the fight/flight survival response and is exactly what should happen. It is not a mistake for blood sugar to increase in such situations; it is natural and even necessary. However, if the situation is not resolved, the survival switch stays turned on too long, the blood sugar level stays high too long, and eventually a diagnosis like diabetes becomes imminent.

It is the same with the thyroid and adrenal glands. These glands work in a similar manner as the accelerator in your car. You press down on the accelerator when you want your car to go faster. A stress message tells the thyroid and adrenal glands to release more hormones to "accelerate" the body so it can flee, "go faster", or fight. If that message never gets turned off, it will always lead to exhaustion since it is not possible to fight or flee forever. The thyroid, adrenals, and body eventually "run out of gas." In Joan's case, even as tired as she was, she still had a difficult time sleeping because of her unresolved situation, and when she did sleep, she never woke up refreshed. Her body was continuing to receive the "go faster" message. The stress kept her body "revved" all the time, even when she was "in park" trying to sleep.

Some stresses can be figured out easily and quickly and only require a fleeting thought, like jumping out of the way of an oncoming car or deciding what to fix for lunch. In these instances the survival switch is turned on, the problem is quickly solved, and the switch is then turned off. This happens almost automatically with hardly any awareness that we are resolving a stress.

Other stresses can be more involved and may require much more mental and emotional effort. Dealing with a frustrating co-worker, not having enough money to pay the bills, having a child with disabilities, or having a husband leave the Church like Joan's did can lead to weeks, months, or years of fearful and worrisome thoughts. Such thoughts cause the mind to race all the time in an emotional fight/flight dilemma. If not resolved, insomnia, anxiety, and panic attacks like Joan experienced could easily begin to occur. The heavier the mental and emotional weight of the situation and the longer its duration, the more likely it is that a person will have some kind of a symptom.

RECOGNIZING STRESS AS A CAUSE

Although such physical and mental reactions to stress are very common, we often fail to recognize them as the *cause* of our symptoms. It took Joan a full year to make the connection between her symptoms and her husband leaving the Church. It took Patty ten years before she recognized her seizures were caused by a very stressful work environment. Ronald had a hard time seeing that his neck pain was due to the divorce he was going through. Anna's long struggle with irritable bowel syndrome obscured the fact that it was caused by abuse when she was a child. Angie's depression was a result of her son's death seventeen years earlier. Unresolved or unrelenting stress, such as these people experienced, can be a contributing factor to almost any symptom or condition a person might have. Some symptoms, like high blood pressure or headaches, can be an instant reaction to stress. Some conditions where stress is often a causative factor, like in heart disease and cancer, may not show up for years.

It takes time to heal from both physical and emotional

injury. We expect a cut to heal in a few days and a broken bone to mend in a couple of months. Hurt feelings and broken hearts require healing time as well, and when associated symptoms persist beyond the expected healing time, stress is often the underlying cause. Resolving that stress is the necessary solution. With chronic symptoms lasting longer than three months, stress is almost always a major factor, and taking steps to resolve it must be seriously considered.

Elder Richard G. Scott told of a time early in his career when worry literally made him sick and how he learned to deal with it. "...*Within eight months, I was in the office of a doctor being carefully examined to determine if I had ulcers. For weeks each night I would return home from work with a severe headache, and only after a long, quiet period of isolation could I calm my nerves sufficiently to sleep briefly and return to work the next day. I began to prayerfully consider my plight. It was ridiculous. All I wanted to do was to be a worthy husband and father and carry out honorably my Church and professional assignments. My best efforts produced frustration, worry, and illness. In time, I was prompted to divide mentally and physically, where possible, all of the challenges and tasks and assignments given to me into two categories: First, those for which I had some ability to control and to resolve, I put into a mental basket called "concern." Second, all the rest of the things that were either brought to me or I imagined I had the responsibility to carry out, but over which I had no control, I put in a basket called "worry." I realized I could not change them to any significant degree, so I studiously strove to completely forget them. The items in the "concern" basket were ordered in priority. I conscientiously tried to resolve them to the best of my ability. I realized that I could not always fulfill all of them on schedule or to the degree of competence I desired, but I did my conscientious best.*

"*Occasionally as I sat in my office, I'd feel my stomach muscles tighten and tension overcome me. I would cease whatever activity I was engaged in and with earnest prayer for support, concentrate on relaxing and overcoming the barrier that worry produced in my life. Over a period of time, those efforts were blessed by the Lord. I again came to understand how the*

Lord is willing to strengthen, fortify, guide, and direct every phase of life. The symptoms of illness passed, and I learned to face tasks under pressure" (Scott, To the Lonely and Misunderstood 1982).

Elder L. Tom Perry also shared a way to deal with stress that had worked for him, *"I remember a particular period of my life when I was under unusual stress. There were troubles with my employment, and at the same time, my wife was diagnosed with a life-threatening illness... On days when the stresses and anxieties of our tumultuous life were about to get the best of us, my wife and I found a way to relieve them. We drove to a place just a few miles from our home to get away for a few moments of relief from our troubles, talk, and give emotional comfort to each other... to pause, reflect, and heal"* (Perry 2008). Both Elder Scott and Elder Perry found ways to heal from the stresses in life. We all need to do the same.

GRIEF AND SORROW

In the scriptures we can find several examples of stress affecting a person's health. One of these is the familiar story of Lehi, Sariah, and their sons, Laman and Lemuel, who were very rebellious and gave them much grief. Their situation became very intense on the ship as they sailed to the promised land. Laman and Lemuel tied up Nephi and threatened anyone who tried to help him. The stress of this awful family predicament sent the aging Lehi and Sariah to their sick-beds and nearly to a watery grave. In 1 Nephi 18 we read,

17 Now my father, Lehi, had said many things unto them, and also unto the sons of Ishmael; but, behold, they did breathe out much threatenings against anyone that should speak for me; and my parents being stricken in years, and having suffered much grief because of their children, they were brought down, yea, even upon their sick-beds.

*18 **Because of their grief and much sorrow**, and the iniquity of my brethren, they were brought near even to be carried out of this time to meet their God; yea, their grey hairs were about to be brought down to lie low in the dust; yea, even they were near to be cast with sorrow into a watery grave.*

Lehi and Sariah's grief and sorrow over the actions of

their children brought them down upon their sick-beds and nearly caused their deaths. A great storm arose and continued for four days. It became so bad that when Laman and Lemuel "... *saw that they were about to be swallowed up in the depths of the sea they repented of the thing which they had done, insomuch that they loosed (Nephi)*" (1 Nephi 18:20). When Nephi was set free, the heavy, stressful burden weighing upon Lehi and Sariah was lifted, their health improved, and they did not die at that time.

In this story of Lehi and Sariah, it was the stresses of grief and sorrow that put them in their sick-beds. In the story of Zeezrom, it was sin and guilt that put him in his. Although stress is not the same thing as sin, the effects on the body are similar. Both sin and stress turn on the switch of survival reactions, and if not turned off, they can be the source of physical symptoms, mental symptoms, and poor health. All three of these individuals were dealing with emotionally heavy burdens that needed to be resolved. The switch of survival reactions needed to be turned off for them to heal. Zeezrom turned off his survival switch and changed how his body was responding by repenting, but repentance couldn't help Lehi and Sariah because they were not sinning. Their relief came when the circumstances changed and they were able to see things differently.

CHANGING PERSPECTIVE

Seeing things differently, or changing perspective, can have a profound impact on the body. Zeezrom's burning fever and miraculous healing were a result of how his changed beliefs manifested in his body. If his beliefs had not changed, he never would have experienced the burning fever or the healing through repentance.

Lehi and Sariah's beliefs are also what put them in their sick beds. Their grief and sorrow were caused by their *belief* that Laman and Lemuel were wrong in tying up Nephi, accompanied by their powerlessness to stop their rebellious sons. Had they believed Laman and Lemuel were right in tying up Nephi, they never would have been sick. They would have had anger, not grief toward Nephi if they had felt as Laman and Lemuel did, who said, "*We will not that our younger brother shall be a ruler over us"* (1 Nephi 18:10).

Understandably, their beliefs were not like Laman and Lemuel's. Lehi and Sariah's desire to defend Nephi and stop the internal family fighting was a logical perspective for them to have. It must be understood, however, that their grief and sorrow were a result of their *perspective* of the stressful situation, not the fact that the stressful situation existed!

In this story there are two perspectives, Laman and Lemuel's and Lehi and Sariah's. There is, however, another important perspective that needs to be considered – God's perspective. If Lehi and Sariah had been able to see things through God's eyes, they would have known why He permitted Laman and Lemuel to tie up Nephi and treat him harshly. Heavenly Father was trying to teach Laman and Lemuel a lesson. *"...nevertheless, the Lord did suffer it that he might show forth his power"* (1 Nephi 18:11). He allowed Nephi to suffer at the hands of Laman and Lemuel to teach them *"...that the judgments of God were upon them, and that they must perish save that they should repent of their iniquities"* (1 Nephi 18:15).

God was providing one more opportunity for Laman and Lemuel to repent. Ironically this is exactly what Lehi and Sariah were hoping for in the first place (see 1 Nephi 8:37, 2 Nephi 1:13, 16). They wanted Laman and Lemuel to repent and didn't recognize this crisis as an opportunity for that to happen. However, in the midst of adversity it can be extremely difficult to see things the way God sees them. Nevertheless, it is still the perspective one has in the situation that determines the physical impact on the body. Had Lehi and Sariah been able to see from God's perspective, they would not have grieved to the point of making themselves sick and nearly *"cast with sorrow into a watery grave,"* but how could they have that Godly perspective when they were in the midst of a life-threatening storm watching one of their children suffer, and possibly die, at the hands of some of their other children?

SEEING GOD'S HAND

Jacob is another prophet whose well-being was greatly affected by his perspective of the adverse events in his life. He had been lead to believe that his son Joseph was dead though

Joseph had actually been sold into Egypt by his brothers. When his other sons told him they needed to take his youngest son Benjamin to Egypt to get provisions because of the famine, he wouldn't allow it. He said, *"My son shall not go down with you; for his brother is dead, and he is left alone: if mischief befall him by the way in the which ye go, then shall ye bring down my gray hairs with sorrow to the grave"* (Genesis 42:38).

Jacob believed his son Joseph was dead, and the thought of losing Benjamin as well was more than he could bear. He knew it would kill him. Joseph, however, was actually still alive and had become a ruler in Egypt, under the Pharaoh. Jacob was reacting to what he *believed* was true, not to what was actually true! Once again, we see that it is beliefs that color perspective, whether or not those beliefs are truly valid.

Joseph saw things from a very positive perspective. Although he could have harbored anger and resentment toward his brothers for selling him into Egypt, he saw the hand of the Lord in their circumstances instead. He comforted them and said to them, *"Now therefore be not grieved, nor angry with yourselves, that ye sold me hither: for God did send me before you to preserve life... So now it was not you that sent me hither, but God"* (Genesis 45:5, 8). Joseph could see that being sold into Egypt was all part of a grander, divine plan.

In our day we remember how the early saints were persecuted, hated, and compelled to leave Ohio, Missouri, and Illinois. We might wonder why God permitted such conditions to exist. President Joseph F. Smith taught, *"When we look back to it we see clearly, beyond any possible doubt, that the hand of God was in it... We now see it has resulted in the greatest blessing possible to us and the Church"* (J. F. Smith 1912). Gaining this perspective of seeing God's hand in our lives can profoundly alter how our bodies react to stress.

Many people have been able to improve their health and well-being by accepting a more godlike perspective of their situation. Merissa learned that lesson in a very personal way. She went to a party during her first week of college, accepted a ride home from a young man and was nearly raped. It was an awful, life-altering experience. Health problems soon showed up. Her menstrual cycle became very irregular, and she would bleed for months at a time. She began to have back pain that hardly ever let up. She got married and later had a baby, but she spent most of her pregnancy in bed with complications. When she and her husband decided they wanted a second child, she conceived again but soon after, miscarried. She became pregnant five more times and each pregnancy ended in a miscarriage. Merissa wondered, as any woman would, what was wrong with her and became very frustrated and depressed.

While talking to a friend one day Merissa told her about nearly being raped. She wondered why God had abandoned her in that moment of her life when she was trying to do all the right things. Her friend replied, *"God didn't abandon you. He protected you! You weren't raped!"* Merissa was stunned and immediately humbled. She hadn't looked at it from that perspective before. All of a sudden she could see how God had reached down and stopped a bad experience from becoming a tragic one, and she became extremely grateful. The next morning she woke up for the first time in several years with no pain in her back. Within a month, she was pregnant and experienced a healthy, normal pregnancy. Seeing God's hand in her life allowed Merissa to change her perspective and have her own personal miracle.

THE ATONEMENT PERSPECTIVE

In Moroni 9 we read an epistle from Mormon to his son. He describes the depraved and degenerate condition of the Lamanites and Nephites and some of the horrific atrocities they committed. His letter is another witness that our perspective has a powerful influence over the physical body. He concludes, almost apologetically, by saying,

"My son, be faithful in Christ; and may not the things which I have written grieve thee, to weigh thee down unto death; but may Christ lift thee up, and may his sufferings and death, and the showing his body unto our fathers, and his mercy and long-suffering, and the hope of his glory and of eternal life, rest in your mind forever" (Moroni 9:25).

Mormon states that the gruesome things he has been talking about are capable of weighing a person all the way down to death, reminiscent of Lehi, Sariah, and Jacob's reactions to their stressful circumstances. The antidote Mormon prescribes is hope in the atonement. Faith in Christ is a bright solution. No matter how horrendous the situation, our choice to see things through the lens of the atonement is always a perspective that brings peace to the soul and turns off the switch of survival reactions.

Elder Donald L. Hallstrom observed the difference the atonement perspective makes. He spoke of two different couples who had each lost a child. Of the first he said, *"Heartbreak turned to grief, grief turned to anger, anger turned to blame, and blame turned to revenge toward the doctor, whom they held fully responsible..."* Of the second couple he noted, *"(They) were heartbroken. Their grief, however, immediately turned them to the Lord and His Atonement"* (Hallstrom 2010).While the first couple became more and more bitter, the second couple found peace through the atonement. It is not the circumstance that determines our reactions; it is our beliefs and our perspective. A true belief in the atonement of Jesus Christ provides us with a perspective that allows us to see God's hand in any of life's stressful events. That perspective may be very difficult to obtain because it is not the way of the "natural man." However, it is a perspective we need to continually strive for.

Enoch is another prophet whose perspective changed when he chose to see through the lens of the atonement. In a vision he saw all those who would be destroyed in the flood at the time of Noah. *"And as Enoch saw this, he had bitterness of soul, and wept over his brethren, and said unto the heavens: I will refuse to be comforted"* (Moses 7:44). Many of these "brethren" were his descendants. It must have seemed horrendous to him that so many people, including his own family, would become so wicked and that God would destroy them all. It is easy to appreciate why he would refuse to be comforted while contemplating such a scene. If he had maintained this perspective, it could have easily put him in his sick-bed. Enoch's attitude changed, however, when the Lord showed him in a vision how Christ would redeem man from sin and death *"...and his soul rejoiced"* (Moses 7:45-47). When Enoch saw what Christ would do his whole perspective changed. What had been so difficult to bear only a moment before was joyfully swallowed up in the miraculous atonement.

No matter who we are, prophets, parents, or children, we must all learn the same lesson for good physical, mental, emotional, and spiritual health – in the stresses of life, we find relief and healing through the atonement of Jesus Christ.

CHANGING FALSE BELIEFS

Like Zeezrom, Lehi, Sariah, Jacob, Joseph, and Enoch, we all have beliefs that determine our perspective. We are not born with those beliefs; rather, they are all learned. We come into this world with a mind that is like an empty hard drive on a computer waiting to be programmed. The experiences that we have, along with the examples and words of parents, siblings, and other people, program our hard drive. Those experiences and teachings make up our belief system and give us a perspective that we inherently believe is correct and true. Because we innately believe our perspective is correct, we will always act on and defend the perspective and beliefs that we have for that is what is natural to us. President Gordon B. Hinckley said, *"As we all know, our lives are guided in large measure by our perceptions"* (Hinckley 1990). We will act on those perceptions until, for some reason, they are changed. Then we will act on and defend our new beliefs and perceptions. Defending those beliefs in any way, whether or not they are actually true, always produces defensive, survival responses in

> ### Krystal's Story
> Krystal had dry eyes. For 10 years they burned, itched, and were always red. Her ophthalmologist said they were the worst case he had ever seen. After Krystal understood that stress could be a factor, she said, *"I became pregnant back then, and my boyfriend left me. I cried for a long time. I finally decided that crying didn't help, and I would not cry anymore."*
> Although difficult to do, Krystal changed her perspective on this stressful memory. She forgave her boyfriend and herself, and her eyes returned to normal.

the body. If those survival reactions are not switched off, manifestation of symptoms in the body becomes inevitable.

Once Nephi was untied, Lehi and Sariah's level of stress decreased which turned off survival reactions and reflected in their improved health. Jacob's stress decreased when he found out Joseph was still alive, and his health likely improved as well. A change in circumstances, or additional information, can make a big difference in our perspective and thus a big difference in our health. That can be good or bad depending on whether the survival switch is being turned on or off.

There are three ways our beliefs and perspectives are changed:

1. **By a change in circumstances** – such as Nephi being untied.
2. **By additional information** – such as finding out Joseph was alive.
3. **By conscious choice** – such as seeing God's hand in the experience.

We can look at another situation that Lehi and Sariah found themselves in and see how beliefs affected perspectives. Lehi had a vision that told him to send his sons back to Jerusalem to get the brass plates. However, the four boys were gone longer than expected, and Sariah believed they must have died in the wilderness. She was quite upset with her husband for having sent them. We read in 1 Nephi 5 how her beliefs and perspective changed until she finally had her own testimony of their mission.

Nephi writes, *"Sariah... truly had mourned because of us. For she had supposed that we had perished in the wilderness; and she also had complained against my father, telling him that he was a visionary man; saying: Behold thou hast led us forth from the land of our inheritance, and my sons are no more, and we perish in the wilderness"* (1 Nephi 5:1-2).

From Sariah's perspective, things were bad and her sons were dead. Lehi was able to comfort her with a different perspective that lightened her load. Because of his vision, he was able to say, *"I know that the Lord will deliver my sons out of the hands of Laban, and bring them down again unto us in the wilderness.* (1 Nephi 5:5).

When Nephi and his brothers returned to their parents, Sariah's perspective was changed even more. She now had a knowledge that God had truly been leading her husband and was able to testify, *"Now I know of a surety that the Lord hath commanded my husband to flee into the wilderness; yea, and I also know of a surety that the Lord hath protected my sons, and delivered them out of the hands of Laban, and given them power whereby they could accomplish the thing which the Lord hath commanded them"* (1 Nephi 5:8). She now had her own testimony of their mission and the same perspective and belief as her husband. We never read of her questioning their journey again. Sariah progressed from complaining about their difficult situation, to being comforted because she believed in Lehi's words, to having her own testimony of their mission all because her beliefs and perspective changed. She had by letting go of judgment and pride.

JUDGMENT AND PRIDE

Judgment and **Pride** are two huge obstacles we must overcome to see things differently and change the false beliefs and perspectives we have. When we make judgments, we are choosing how we see things; we are reflecting our perspective. Pride can follow judgment and is a defensive reaction according to the perspective we have chosen to believe.

*Bella had suffered off and on with sciatic pain in her leg and for two years it had been especially constant. She realized her leg pain originally began fifteen years earlier at a very stressful time in her life when a new employee had been hired at her place of employment, and Bella had found her very difficult to work with. "In fact," Bella added, "No one could get along with her!" This employee had also been very mean to Bella's daughter and had done some things to her Bella **could never forgive her for**. Bella also realized that while on a senior mission two years earlier, she had been assigned a companion that was very irritating and difficult to get along with. Her sciatic pain had increased in severity then and had grown even worse since that assignment.*

139

Bella was able to rid herself of chronic leg pain by forgiving these two people and forgiving herself, but she had to overcome judgment and pride to do that. At first she didn't want to forgive them because she felt they were at fault. When she realized it was her judgmental feelings toward these women that were *causing* her pain, it became easier to forgive and move on.

Bella had judged these women as "mean" and "irritating" and that was not her right. She was falling into the trap that President Dieter F. Uchtdorf warned about, *"When it comes to our own prejudices and grievances, we too often justify our anger as righteous and our judgment as reliable and only appropriate. Though we cannot look into another's heart, we assume that we know a bad motive or even a bad person when we see one. We make exceptions when it comes to our own bitterness because we feel that, in our case, we have all the information we need to hold someone else in contempt"* (Uchtdorf 2012). President Uchtdorf's words describe Bella's perspective perfectly. She believed her judgment of these other women was right and appropriate, so she was able to hold them *"in contempt."* She didn't realize, however, that such a judgment would result in fifteen years of leg pain.

We are taught in the scriptures and by church leaders that we are to love all men and not judge them. Elder Dallin H. Oaks gave additional instruction on judgment, *"Whenever possible we will **refrain from judging people and only judge situations.** This is essential whenever we attempt to act upon different standards than others with whom we must associate – at home, at work or in the community"* (Oaks 1999). Bella was not only judging situations she was in, she was also judging people. The defensive reaction of pride naturally followed, turning on her survival switch with sciatic pain as a symptom.

President Ezra Taft Benson taught of two ways that pride manifests itself. They are:

1. *"We pit our will against God's... it is in the spirit of '**my will and not thine be done**...' We are tempted daily to elevate ourselves above others and diminish them"* (E. T. Benson 1989). This was Bella's attitude. She had elevated herself above others by judging

them in a negative way. She needed to repent of that prideful attitude to be free of its spiritual and physical effects upon her.

2. *"The proud stand more in fear of men's judgment than of God's judgment. 'What will men think of me?' weighs heavier than 'What will God think of me?'"* (E. T. Benson 1989). This second form of pride is much more subtle and much more common for most of us. It manifests itself in the form of feelings of inadequacy or feelings of being judged or rejected by others. It is found even among the prophets. Moroni worried because he didn't think he was a good writer, *"... when we write we behold our weakness, and stumble because of the placing of our words; and I fear lest the Gentiles shall mock at our words"* (Ether 12:23). Moses questioned his ability to lead the Israelites, *"Who am I... that I should bring forth the children of Israel out of Egypt?... they will not believe me, nor hearken unto my voice"* (Exodus 3:11, 4:1). Joseph Smith gave Martin Harris the 116 page manuscript which Martin ultimately lost and Joseph was reprimanded by the Lord because *"...(he) should not have feared man more than God"* (D&C 3:7).

If feelings of inadequacy or being judged or rejected persist, then physical symptoms are bound to follow. Heidi experienced this rejection when her sister told her she didn't want to associate with Heidi and her family any more. Heidi was devastated by this announcement. It consumed her, and she didn't know how to respond. Nine months later Heidi had stomach troubles, insomnia, no energy, and was depressed. Although Heidi's feelings are understandable to all of us, allowing them to persist was destructive to both her and her family. There was only so much she could do to try to mend her relationship with her sister. She is like Nephi who prayed to fix his relationship with Laman and Lemuel, without success; it only got worse. In 2 Nephi 5 we read,

1 Behold, it came to pass that I, Nephi, did cry much unto the Lord my God, because of the anger of my brethren.

2 But behold, their anger did increase against me, insomuch that they did seek to take away my life…

5 And it came to pass that the Lord did warn me, that I, Nephi, should depart from them and flee into the wilderness, and all those who would go with me.

Nephi's answer was to separate himself from his brothers. Heidi needed to find out what God would have her do as well. In terms of President Benson's words, *"What will (my sister) think of me?"* weighed heavier on her than *"what will God think of me?"* If she turned to Heavenly Father and received an answer from Him, then she could be at peace, no matter the outcome of the situation.

These two forms of pride, the need to be right and the fear of what others think, produce defensive, survival reactions in the body and eventually symptoms if we do not let them go. President Uchtdorf prescribed a perfect antidote, *"We simply have to stop judging others and replace judgmental thoughts and feelings with a heart full of love for God and His children"* (Uchtdorf 2012). Bella recognized how judgment and pride had contributed to the pain in her leg and that she needed to forgive to get well. Heidi came to understand how a *"heart full of love for God and (her sister)"* allowed her to forgive and see things differently. Her symptoms improved even though her relationship with her sister didn't. She chose to love God and her sister enough to trust that God would help mend their relationship someday. Bella and Heidi were both able to change their perceptions and their symptoms went away. We also have a choice in how we see things.

BE OF GOOD CHEER

We can see things with an eye of faith or with an eye of fear. Fear comes to us naturally. It is part of our survival instinct and is common to the natural man. Faith, in contrast, is a spiritual perspective that comes with choice and effort. The spiritual must overcome the natural to see things with an eye of faith. Elder Quentin L. Cook taught, *"Our doctrine is clear; we are to be positive and of good cheer. We emphasize our faith, not our fears. We rejoice in the Lord's assurance that He will stand by us and give us guidance and direction"* (Cook 2012).Such a perspective has a direct impact on our health.

Millie's father passed away when she was 6 years old. She always felt that his premature death was unfair and that she had been "cheated." Her mother remarried when Millie was 14, but Millie did not get along with her step-father. That only magnified the unfairness of her father's death. When Millie was 65, her husband passed away. The "cheated" emotions that she felt as a child with the loss of her father resurfaced. She began to have restless leg syndrome which allowed her very little sleep at night for the next four years. Then, she learned that her emotions could have a great impact on her physically and how and why she needed to change her perspective, so Millie chose to change her beliefs. She chose to see God's hand in what had happened in her life rather than feeling life was unfair. She chose to be grateful for the years she'd had with her husband and the time she had spent with her father. She saw that time as a blessing rather than feeling she'd been cheated. That change of belief and perspective turned off the survival switch and allowed her restlessness to end, and she once again could sleep

Marie's Experience

"In body and spirit I was sick, wounded, and truly felt that I would not survive the pain of loss.

One afternoon I came home and found that my young son had died, taking his own life. He was 15 years old. I spent sleepless nights that stretched to weeks and months, wondering how I could survive feeling so lonely, afraid, sick, oppressed, and brokenhearted.

*"I recall reading 'What I say unto one I say unto all, **be of good cheer**, little children; for I am in your midst, and I have not forsaken you'* (D&C 61:36). *I remember the spirit whispering to me that that meant me too.*

"I found I had much to be joyful for. I can bear testimony from personal experience that the Lord does indeed answer prayers."

comfortably at night.

As a six-year-old Millie's perspective of her father dying is understandable and natural. However, at some point that perspective needed to change because she couldn't carry that "unfair" belief her whole life without it creating a survival reaction in her body. The addition of her husband's death or any other "unfair situations" only made things worse.

Elder Jeffrey R. Holland taught about the kind of perspective we should all strive to have, *"The spirit of the gospel is optimistic; it trusts in God and looks on the bright side of things."* He then added, *"We should honor the Savior's declaration to "be of good cheer" (Indeed, it seems to me we may be more guilty of breaking that commandment than almost any other!)"* (Holland 2007). Being optimistic and of good cheer turns off the switch of survival reactions; then better health and improved well-being naturally follow. As we strive to *walk in obedience to all the commandments*, we receive the promised blessings of the Word of Wisdom. Being of good cheer is one of the most helpful commandments in overcoming the stresses of life.

PROGRAMMED PATTERNS

Symptoms that last for months or years, like Millie's restless leg syndrome, often indicate a programmed pattern or response in the body for handling the fears and worries of stressful events and situations. We learn how to react to events just like we learn to ride a bike or tie a shoe. Our physical reactions become automatic and normal, whether or not we "approve" of them. A chronic symptom is often just a learned pattern of response to stress. It continues until the pattern is changed by seeing the stress differently in some way.

Fran got engaged in June and then broke off her engagement in August. It was a very stressful experience, and her fiancé did not handle it well. Every August for the next 10 years, Fran's nose and sinuses would plug up making it difficult to breathe. Her "allergy" would last for two months and then go away.

When Fran learned that her August allergy could be due to a negative memory, she decided she needed to try to see it differently. She thought about how much worse things could have been and how grateful she was that things had turned out so well. She was able to see God's hand in the experience and how he had blessed her. She forgave her fiancé and herself and recognized that she had learned an important lesson about trusting Heavenly Father. Fran was able to overcome her "allergy" by "re-programming" the stressful memory of breaking up with her boyfriend. She turned off the switch of survival reactions that had stayed on for 10 years and didn't experience "allergies" again.

Programmed patterns of symptoms are often the result of negative reactions to stressful situations that our beliefs and perspective tell us are wrong or undesirable. If we handle it in a Christ-like way as we work through it, the survival switch will get turned off. If we handle it in less than a Christ-like way, the survival switch stays turned on and may lead to symptoms that chronically plague us. We fix the "faulty switch" with faith as we let go of fear.

Annette's Story

"I averaged two migraines a month. I changed my diet and tried many other things, but never could get rid of them. One day I was watching General Conference and was feeling really good. Then a program came on about the family. I soon had a migraine. I realized the trigger to my migraines was when I wished I had been a better mom and I knew I needed to forgive myself to break that pattern."

Elder Jeffrey R. Holland described the solution, *"The formula of faith is to hold on, work on, see it through, and let the distress of earlier hours—real or imagined—fall away in the abundance of the final reward. Don't dwell on old issues or grievances—not toward yourself nor your neighbor nor even, I might add, toward this true and living Church. We consume such precious emotional and spiritual capital clinging tenaciously to the memory of a discordant note we struck in a childhood piano recital, or something a spouse said or did 20 years ago that we are determined to hold over his or her head for another 20"*

(Holland 2012).

When a memory is consuming "precious emotional and spiritual capital," forgiving ourselves for striking the discordant note as a child or forgiving our spouse for something he or she said 20 years ago can literally improve our health Such memories keep our survival switch turned on, but faith and forgiveness are keys to turning it off. Oftentimes, however, the hardest part of getting well is not exercising faith or forgiveness; it is knowing what or who we need to forgive or what experience caused the symptoms to appear in the first place.

EMOTIONAL IDENTIFIERS

Identifying the emotional cause of our symptoms is an extremely important part of healing from stress induced health conditions. Fran needed to identify that the stress of breaking up with her fiancé caused her allergies. Millie needed to see that the death of both her husband and her father were contributing to her restless legs. We need to identify the causes so we can fix them with faith, forgiveness, and/or repentance. There are six Emotional Identifiers of Symptoms (Wilde 2011) that can help us discover which of our stresses are contributing to the health problems we have.

1. **Current Stress** – anything in the present you think about often, like Lehi and Sariah's stress over their sons that brought them to their sick beds.

2. **When Symptoms Began** – think of what was stressful in your life when symptoms first started, like Fran breaking up with her fiancé 10 years earlier that caused her allergies.

3. **Vivid Memories** – think of a vivid memory of an event or something said or felt. When you think of the memory, the emotions are strong and the mental picture of the situation is vivid, like Millie's memory at age six when her dad died.

4. **Undesirable Events** – think of something that happened that you wish hadn't happened, like Merissa's near rape in college that lead to several miscarriages.

5. **Unresolved Situations** – think of something in your life that is still unresolved, like Jim's ongoing lawsuit that caused him chronic back pain.

6. **Prayer and Scriptures** – pray and read your scriptures to seek the Lord's help in identifying the *cause* of your health problems. This can also help you discover the solution. President Henry B. Eyring described one way to do this, *"Sometimes I go to the scriptures for instruction. I go with a question, and the question usually is 'What would God have me do?' or 'What would God have me feel?' Invariably I find new ideas, thoughts I have never had before, and I receive inspiration and instruction and answers to my questions... Going to the scriptures to learn what to do makes all the difference. The Lord can teach us. When we come to a crisis in our life, such as losing a child or spouse, we should go looking in the scriptures for specific help. We will find answers in the scriptures. The Lord seemed to anticipate all of our problems and all of our needs, and He put help in the scriptures for us - if only we seek it"* (Eyring 2005).

Elder Richard G. Scott described a similar pattern that he uses to obtain answers from the scriptures. We can use his approach to identify emotional *causes* of the health issues we have. He said, *"When I am faced with a very difficult matter, this is how I try to understand what to do. I fast. I pray to find and understand scriptures that will be helpful. That process is cyclical. I start reading a passage of scripture; I ponder what the verse means and pray for inspiration. I then ponder and pray to know if I have captured all the Lord wants me to do. Often more impressions come with increased understanding of doctrine. I have found that pattern to be a good way to learn from the scriptures"* (Scott 2012). (For more information on finding answers and direction in the scriptures, see the author's book *The Liahona Principle.*)

The stresses of life have a much bigger impact on our health than most of us realize. We often need to handle them better in order to heal and be well.

THE BIG PICTURE

As we deal with stress, we need to keep in mind the big picture, that the stresses of life are a proving ground. The Lord tells us the purpose of life in Abraham 3:25, *"And we will prove them herewith, to see if they will do all things whatsoever the Lord their God shall command them"*. Commenting on this verse, President Henry B. Eyring said, *"The great test of life is to see whether we will hearken to and obey God's commands in the midst of the storms of life. It is not to endure storms, but to choose the right while they rage"* (Eyring 2005). Whether the "storms of life" are small or great, there is a correct and proper way to handle them, which is the Christ-like way. President Howard W. Hunter taught, *"Let us follow the Son of God in all ways and in all walks of life... We should at every opportunity ask ourselves, "What would Jesus do?" and then be more courageous to act upon the answer. We must follow Christ, in the best sense of that word. We must be about his work as he was about his Father's. We should try to be like him"* (Hunter 1994).

If we can see the big picture, the stress we are dealing with shrinks in size. We are able to see that our stressful situation is really a lesson to help us learn to be more Christ-like. It is teaching us to be more patient, kind, loving, thoughtful, understanding, meek, humble – more like our Savior. The better we learn these lessons, the better our health will generally be. With the right perspective, the switch of survival reactions does not get turned on, or at least if it does, it doesn't stay on as long.

Betty lost eighty-five percent of the vision in her right eye. She had an inflamed optic nerve and was told she would likely go blind in that eye. For ten years she had problems seeing with that eye, but then one morning she awakened with a severe loss of vision.

Betty's aged mother had cancer and was taking care of Betty's brother who had Multiple Sclerosis. Betty could see the toll this was taking on her mother and suggested different arrangements. Her mother disagreed with Betty's suggestions, saying her only reason for living was to care for her son. Betty was worried about her mother and brother but felt helpless. Love and a sense of obligation had Betty convinced that it was her responsibility to do something. She couldn't sit back and watch things get worse, yet it seemed she didn't have any other choice.

This stressful circumstance weighed heavily on Betty until it literally affected her ability to see. She finally concluded there was nothing she could do to change the situation and turned it over to God. She recognized that she needed to love her mother and brother in their present circumstances and not try to change them. She would give them help and support when the

Naomi's Story

Naomi was diagnosed with adrenal insufficiency at age fifteen. She would come home after school, go to bed, eat supper, and go back to bed. She could sleep all the time. She was placed on steroid drugs to help with the exhaustion and had been taking them for twenty years.

Naomi remembered that when she was fifteen, her mother was diagnosed with AIDS. Naomi was "deflated" by the news and knew that life would not be simple any more.

Now, Naomi was able to look at the big picture and see God's hand in how her family was blessed at that time. As she maintained that perspective, her energy level significantly improved and eventually she was able to go off the steroids.

opportunity arose.

As Betty chose to see things differently, her vision literally improved. Within two weeks, it improved sixty percent in the affected eye. Two years later, it was ninety-five percent normal, and she could see better out of her right eye than her left.

Betty acknowledged errors in many aspects of her thinking. She had to learn to let go of the desire to control everything so it turned out the way she thought it should. She realized that it was all right if the people around her made mistakes. It was okay that her brother had MS. It was all right that her dad died. Her mother had a right to choose how to spend her time and energy. With Heavenly Father's help, Betty was able to change her perspective. Her solution was to see the big picture. God was in charge and he would help her. By having faith in the big picture, she was able to let go. Her body was then able to do what it had been programmed to automatically do – be healthy.

THY WILL BE DONE

Sometimes pain, suffering, and death are necessary outcomes. Our Heavenly Father sees the big picture and understands so much more than we do. A situation we may perceive as a horrible tragedy may not be that in the eyes of the Lord. Our Heavenly Father sees all and understands all. We must trust that He will strengthen us in our trials and influence outcomes for our best good, according to His wisdom. We may need to humble ourselves as we trust God, exercise faith in the big picture, and acknowledge to him "Thy will be done."

In the following story Jason struggled to learn how to say *"Thy will be done"* and truly mean it. Most of us can relate in some way to his story through experiences that are personal and unique to us.

"My wife and I attended a child birth class in which a nutritionist commented that all of us have cancer cells in our bodies, and depending on the quality of our nutrition, those cancer cells will either be able to take over our bodies or our bodies will be able to fight off the cancerous cells. That was it. It was a very short comment that came in passing, but it had a

tremendous impact on me.

About three weeks later, I noticed a very slight throbbing in a part of my body. For some reason, my mind immediately grabbed hold of the idea that I PROBABLY (I skipped right over possibly) had cancer. My mind locked in on this idea, and I could think of nothing else. I started losing sleep. My appetite shrunk to almost nothing. I was filled with fear, dread, and terror for days. I prayed and read my scriptures but the comfort was only momentary.

I read a General Conference talk by Elder Richard G. Scott in which he taught that until we get to the point of saying, "Thy will be done" when praying to the Lord in the midst of a trial, that we are not able to fully draw down the powers of heaven to bless our lives (Richard G. Scott, "Trust in the Lord," Ensign, Nov. 1995, 16). This struck me because I had never felt so engulfed in utter dread and terror. I knew that I needed all the blessings the Savior could bestow upon me; however, I had felt too scared to pray that the Lord's will would be done. I was worried that His will would result in my death from cancer.

Finally, in a quiet moment I knelt down and with a trembling heart, I prayed those words, 'Thy will be done!" I felt so nervous to do it. I almost felt that I was giving the Lord permission to take my life right then and there. I was so worried about who would take care of my wife and my soon-to-be-born daughter.

I would like to say that upon uttering this prayer my discomfort, terror, dread, and fear vanished and I was left to bask in peace and joy. It was not like that for me. I thought that this was such a cruel affliction because while the physical pain and discomfort were exceptionally minor, the mental, emotional, and spiritual burdens were exceedingly heavy and wearying. The mental games were almost more than I could bear. I didn't know how to remove this dread and worry from my mind. I was trying to replace my fear with faith, and I was praying that the Lord's will would be done, but I didn't know how to feel okay with whatever the Lord's will would be. Saying, "Thy will be done" and really, whole-heartedly believing those words was proving to be more than I could handle.

Throughout this difficulty, I kept turning to the Book of

Mormon and asking the Lord what I should learn and what I should do. Over and over the verses I turned to kept telling me to repent. I knew that I needed to repent of this extreme lack of mental and emotional faith, but I didn't know how to remove this sin from my mind. Trusting in the Lord's answers has proven to be the most difficult aspect of this experience. I feel comfort for a moment, but then the world rushes in and takes over with feelings of doubt and fear. It took a long two months to learn that I did indeed need to do my part, and that it was only through me doing my part that I could replace my mental fear with faith. I had to start thinking of others and their needs, I had to cut out mentally wasting activities such as television, and I had to stop doing things that would cause me to recall my cancer fears (such as constantly checking myself for cancerous growths and researching it online).

What I have finally begun to learn is that the Lord will not lie to us. Indeed the answers that I received from the beginning have been the answers that were best for me. I needed to trust in the Savior and recognize how this experience has prepared me for a greater work. I count myself lucky to have had this affliction.

No matter our trial or affliction, if we can see it with an eye of faith and trust in God, it will be a blessing to us. God's will, **will** be done, whether we accept it or not. Elder Richard G. Scott said, *"Your willingness to accept the will of the Father will not change what in His wisdom He has chosen to do. However, it will certainly change the effect of those decisions on you personally"* (Scott, Trust in the Lord 1995). When we humbly accept God's will in our, we will be at peace, our switch of survival reactions will turn off, and we will be blessed with an optimal potential for good health..

SUMMARY: VARIABLE O – OBEDIENCE TO THE COMMANDMENTS

The third variable in the Word of Wisdom Formula is *Walking in Obedience to the Commandments*. In order to receive the promised temporal and spiritual blessings we need to:

1. Obey all the Commandments by:
- Repenting and being free from sin.
- Learning how to handle stress in a Christ-like way.

THE WORD OF WISDOM FORMULA			
KEEP THE DON'TS +	DO THE DO'S +	OBEDIENCE TO COMMANDMENTS =	PROMISED BLESSINGS

11

THE WORD OF WISDOM FORMULA FOR HEALTH AND HEALING

The Word of Wisdom is a very remarkable revelation about what we can do to have good physical, mental, emotional, and spiritual health. There is no document anywhere that compares. It comes from a loving Heavenly Father who is concerned about our *"temporal salvation,"* as well as our spiritual salvation, and is adapted to the *"capacity of the weak and weakest"* among us (see D&C 89:2-3). The difficulty in living it lies not in its rules but in the many alternative choices available to us. He created the bodies He endowed us with and gave us the Word of Wisdom as an "Owner's Manual" to help keep them in their best working condition. It is a powerful revelation because it ties principles to promises and allows us our agency to choose the degree of blessings we receive.

This book has attempted to show how the degree of health blessings we receive *varies* according to our understanding and obedience to these principles. Let's look at these wonderful blessings again (D&C 89:18-21).

18. ... shall receive health in their navel and marrow to their bones.

19. And shall find wisdom and great treasures of knowledge, even hidden treasures.

20. And shall run and not be weary, and shall walk and not faint.

21. And I, the Lord, give unto them a promise, that the destroying angel shall pass by them, as the children of Israel, and not slay them. Amen.

These marvelous promises are available to all of us if we obey the principles which qualify us to receive them. The more we are able to *keep the don'ts*, *do the do's*, and *walk in obedience to the commandments*, the greater our ability to receive the promised blessings.

I have put these principles in the form of a formula to illustrate our role in receiving these blessings. There is a responsibility on our part that cannot be ignored if we desire good health. We must do what the Lord requires of us on the left side of the equation if we desire to receive all He has to offer us on the right.

Here is the Word of Wisdom Formula in its entirety and a summary of what each variable means.

THE WORD OF WISDOM FORMULA			
KEEP THE DON'TS	+ DO THE DO'S	+ OBEDIENCE TO COMMANDMENTS	= PROMISED BLESSINGS

VARIABLE K – KEEPING THE DON'TS
1. Abstain from the specific don'ts of tea, coffee, tobacco, alcohol and illegal drugs.
2. Abstain from other don'ts revealed to us by experience, study and through the Spirit.

VARIABLE D – DOING THE DO'S
1. **Food Group 1 – Herbs** – Eat lots of vegetables and legumes.
2. **Food Group 2 – Fruit** – Eat lots of fruit and some nuts.

3. **Food Group 3 – Meat Sparingly** – Eat sparingly of meats and dairy.
4. **Food Group 4 – Grain** – Eat lots of whole grains.

VARIABLE O – OBEDIENCE TO THE COMMANDMENTS

1. Obey all the Commandments by:
- Repenting and being free from sin.
- Learning how to handle stress in a Christ-like way.

TESTIMONIALS

For over 30 years I have watched people apply these principles in their lives to heal and improve their health. Some have made small changes and others have made large ones. Some have made changes in only one of the variables and some have made them in all three. Invariably the status and quality of their health is a reflection of how well they *keep the don'ts, do the do's* and *walk in obedience to the commandments*. Their health and wellness is not a function of chance but of choice. We are all the same, so if we desire better health, then we need to make better choices on our side of the equation. Below are some more stories of people who have healed and/or improved their health by choosing to more closely follow the inspired principles of the Word of Wisdom.

Nancy has closely followed the 4 Food Groups of the Word of Wisdom for the past 10 years. She ate mostly whole plant foods, animal products only occasionally, and tried to avoid all foods with white flour, sugar, and added chemicals. Nancy said, *"Every physical ailment I had has disappeared over the past ten years – most recently plantar warts. One spring day I went out and shoveled dirt all day. I was very tired that evening and expected to be extremely sore the next day, but I didn't have any soreness at all. It was amazing!"*

Tony hurt his back when he fell moving a refrigerator. For the next eight years, he suffered from low back pain and a feeling in his ankles and feet of *"being on fire."* He had cortisone shots in his back and a procedure to cauterize the nerves in his lumbar discs to block the pain which had little effect. He said if he took pain medication twice a day his pain level was 3-5 on a scale of 10. If he forgot to take it, it would quickly jump to a 7. When Tony learned that stress could be causing his symptoms, he was skeptical. However, he knew he had a lot of anger with his employer over the refrigerator incident. He worked on forgiveness and tried to see God's hand in what had happened, and he experienced an immediate sense of relief. That encouraged him, so he worked on forgiving and letting go of blame with that incident and several others that weighed on him. His symptoms improved. Two months later he was off all pain medications, and for the first time in eight years, he had no pain in his back. When the back pain returned, which it occasionally did, he was able to relate it to something stressful and then work on that issue. (Note: Tony smoked a pack of cigarettes a day and was a fairly heavy coffee drinker, so he still had changes he could make that would further improve his health.)

———

Melia was diagnosed with leukemia at age 18. During the healing process she went from being totally exhausted and bed-ridden to running marathons. She describes the lessons she learned as she incorporated the principles of the Word of Wisdom with her medical treatment.

"The first two years of having cancer were definitely a struggle to endure. I relied on my Savior so much more in those two years, however, than any other time thus far in my life. I feel like I began to learn how important it is to help others, to pray for others, and to serve others. I learned that it's important not to judge others. People - friends, family, teachers, and strangers - all deal with things we do not know about.

"I've concluded thus far that a whole-foods, plant based diet is best and one that will help me to naturally heal myself. I

try to eat foods in their natural, raw form as much as possible and try to avoid processed foods. Last summer for a month I ate zero white flour and zero white sugar which resulted in virtually eliminating processed foods from my diet. I ate mostly fruits and vegetables along with some grains and a little meat. At the end of that month, I felt the best I could ever remember feeling. I have found that the body is so forgiving. As soon as we start to put good things into it, it gives us good results. The more I experiment with a healthy diet, the more I see the great benefits of it. I honestly believe that through diet especially, and a healthy lifestyle, my body has the ability to heal itself. I just have to give it the right tools to do so."

Kimberly's Story – *"For a whole week out of each month I could barely function due to female problems. My hands and feet were always cold, and I'd had kidney infections on and off for years. My right arm and leg were usually numb and constipation was a way of life for me for as long as I could remember. For twenty years I had chronic low back pain, and I also had neck pain for ten years from a whiplash injury. My energy was so low I could hardly do more than sit in a chair most of the day. I felt life was closing in around me, and I was usually depressed or sad.*

*Then I learned about living **all** the principles of the Word of Wisdom. That was the beginning of the journey that has helped me to find healing, happiness, and peace. My neck pain, numbness, and kidney infections were the first to get better. Eventually the constipation, low back pain, and female problems completely went away. Even though I thought my diet was good, I realized some of the things I was eating were contributing to my ailments. I learned a better way to deal with stress in my life. As I ate better and thought better, I felt more energy, happiness, and hope. I am grateful for the Word of Wisdom, and I feel certain that anyone can be helped by following its principles, regardless of their condition."*

Sandra's Story – *"I had fibromyalgia. I suffered constantly with pain in my elbows, neck, and lower back, and couldn't sleep. It hurt to even carry my purse. I was having a hard time caring for the children in my pre-school. My doctor put me on anti-depressants so that I could sleep and told me to exercise with weights. The anti-depressants gave me a headache, and I wasn't able to sleep. Implementing the positive aspects of the Word of Wisdom has brought my fibromyalgia under control. I have found that the most important part of controlling my fibromyalgia is being able to sleep, and I have been able to accomplish this as a result of this approach. I eat much better, have a more positive mental outlook and can accept things as they are. This helps me to relax, sleep well, and feel great."*

Carol's Story – *"Shortness of breath, stress, loss of hope, heart disease, COPD, high blood pressure, high cholesterol - I'd had these symptoms as well as anxiety, nervousness and poor digestion for at least five years. I was on oxygen twenty-four hours a day and had to use a nebulizer four times a day. My back and chest hurt continually. Just to breathe was severely painful. I had three stents, a pacemaker, and was on numerous medications. I'd had three heart attacks and was confined to my home most of the time.*

"The Word of Wisdom Formula for Health and Healing has made a huge difference for me. My back pain is totally gone! What a relief that is! For the first time that I can remember, my back does not hurt. My cholesterol level is now at 162. I no longer need my nebulizer and am only using my oxygen at night, and sometimes I don't even need it then. I now feel energized and full of hope! I've had marvelous emotional breakthroughs which have made me feel like a 100 pound burden has been lifted off my back. HEALING!! That is the most precious word to me. I was told four times that I was dying. I will continue to apply the Word of Wisdom principles because I want to get well. I believe wholeheartedly that I can."

Ed's Story – *"I injured my back shoveling which eventually lead to back surgery. The operation was a failure, and I lived with constant pain for a year after that. After an epidural and a nerve deadening surgery, which also didn't help, my neurosurgeon finally threw up his hands in despair and said there was nothing more he could do. That's when I put into practice the principles of the Word of Wisdom Formula. After six weeks, my back was significantly better. I have learned why my back pain comes and am shedding layers of stress and tension. Before the back trouble, I had seven heart surgeries and nearly died from a surgery to remove a portion of my colon and intestines. I am continually feeling lighter and happier as I deal with the root of my health problems. Even my children have commented that Dad seems much happier and content."*

Laura's Story – *"My story is of my issues with carpal tunnel and how my diet affects this ongoing symptom. Being a graphic designer, I've had wrist and arm pain for at least seven years. In January of 2009, I took on a new task involving data entry at work. I spent many hours each day doing repetitive keyboard sequences, and by that summer, my carpal tunnel symptoms were so bad I thought I would have to quit my job. I did some physical therapy and chiropractic work on my shoulder but things were not improving, so I opted for carpal tunnel surgery. It took about six months after the surgery to work without pain.*

"However, about a year after that, the same issues started up again... tense shoulder, sore wrists and thumb. It was not as bad as before the surgery, but it was troublesome. In October 2011 I began to eat a near vegan diet. I eliminated nearly all meat, dairy, and animal products, as well as white flour and white sugar and ate a lot more vegetables. Since I began eating this way, I noticed I can work longer without my wrists hurting. The pain, if any, is very little, and I don't have to baby my arm in the evenings! Now if I do notice my wrist hurts, I can always connect it to the fact that I have been eating animal products lately (I have been a sucker for cheeseburgers!). It's a

great reminder to stick to the diet! In addition, sticking to the Word of Wisdom gives me so much energy and combats depression. When I'm on a healthy path, I feel good about myself and am not as irritated or stressed out by situations. There's a clarity and focus I am able to achieve - the house is cleaner, things are better organized, and my freelance work is more productive. I'm able to be a better friend/mother to others when I don't have my own stressors distracting me. I would recommend the diet to anyone."

CONCLUSION

The body is the most marvelous creation on earth. The Word of Wisdom is the owner's manual we have been given to keep it in good temporal and spiritual working order. It is a wonderful guide that provides a simple formula to keep us healthy.

I repeat the promise made by Elder John A. Widstoe, *"Conscientious study and application of this law of health, including its positive directions, will permit **all** to (claim these precious blessings)"* (Widstoe 1937). As we *keep the don'ts, do the do's,* and *walk in obedience to the commandments* we will receive the Lord's promised blessings of good health. When we do our part, He does His, and we will be blessed with health, vitality, and energy throughout our entire lives.

Bibliography

Agriculture, U. S. (2000). *Profiling Food Consumption in America.* Retrieved from USDA Factbook: http://www.usda.gov/factbook/chapter2.pdf

Aldana Ph.D., S. (2005). *The Culprit and The Cure.* Mapleton, UT: Maple Mountain Press.

Allen, A. W. (1998, Oct 1). *Feasting with the Prophets.* Retrieved from LDS Church News: http://www.ldschurchnews.com/articles/17785/Feasting-with-the-prophets.html

Andersen, N. L. (2009, November). Repent... That I May Heal You. *Ensign.*

Bailor, J. (2012). *The Smarter Science of Slim.* Aavia Publishing.

Barnard M.D., N. (1993). *Food for Life.* New York: Crown Publishers.

Barzel, U. S., & Massey, L. K. (1998). *Excess Dietary Protein Can Adversely Affect Bone.* Retrieved from The Journal of Nutrition: http://jn.nutrition.org/content/128/6/1051.long

Bednar, D. A. (2008, November). Pray Always. *Ensign.*

Benson, E. T. (1855, Apr 8). *The Word of Wisdom.* Retrieved from scriptures.byu.edu: http://scriptures.byu.edu/jod/jodhtml.php?vol=02&disc=53

Benson, E. T. (1974, Nov). Do Not Despair. *Ensign*, p. 65.

Benson, E. T. (1974, January). Prepare Ye. *Ensign.*

Benson, E. T. (1979). *In His Step.* Retrieved from BYU Speeches:http://speeches.byu.edu/reader/reader.php?id=6718&x=42&y=6

Benson, E. T. (1983, May). A Principle with a Promise. *Ensign*, p. 53.

Benson, E. T. (1989, May). Beware of Pride. *Ensign*, p. 4.

Berge, A. F. (2008). *How the Ideology of Low Fat Conquered America.* Retrieved from Journal of the History of Medicine:http://jhmas.oxfordjournals.org/content/63/2/13 9.short?rss=1&ssource=mfr

Boyer, J., & H Liu, R. (2004). *Apple Phytochemicals and their Health Benefits.* Retrieved from Nutrition Journal: http://www.nutritionj.com/content/3/1/5

Brown, B. (2012, March). *Ted.com - Listening to Shame.* Retrieved from http://www.ted.com/talks/brene_brown_listening_to_sha me.html

Campbell Ph.D., T. C. (2012). *The China Study.* Retrieved from The China Study: http://thechinastudy.com/

Campbell, T. C., & Campbell, T. M. (2006). *The China Study.* Dallas, TX: BenBella Books.

Carlson D.O., J. (2007). *Genocide: How Your Doctor's Dietary Ignorance Will Kill You!!!!* Book Surge Publishing.

Center for Disease Control. (2012). *Protein.* Retrieved from Center for Disease Control: http://www.cdc.gov/nutrition/everyone/basics/protein.htm l#How%20much%20protein

Center for Sustainable Systems. (2011). *US Food System Fact Sheet.* Retrieved from Center for Sustainable Systems: http://css.snre.umich.edu/css_doc/CSS01-06.pdf

Cheng, J. (2000). *Volume of a Human Stomach.* Retrieved 2012, from hypertextbook.com: http://hypertextbook.com/facts/2000/JonathanCheng.shtm l

Clawson, R. (1920). *General Conference.* Retrieved from corpus.byu.edu: http://corpus.byu.edu/gc/?c=gc&q=14313215

Cook, Q. L. (2012, May). In Tune with the Music of Faith. *Ensign.*

Dakota Yeast. (2012). *Yeast Fermentation in Baked Goods.* Retrieved from Dakota Yeast: http://www.dakotayeast.com/help-fermentation.html

Davis, W. (2011). *Wheat Belly.* Rodale.

Decode Me. (2012). *Lactose Intolerance.* Retrieved from decodeme.com: http://www.decodeme.com/lactose-intolerance

Diet Index. (2012). Retrieved from Every Diet: http://www.everydiet.org/diets.htm

Duncan, A. W. (1905). *The Chemistry of Food and Nutrition.* Plain Label Books.

Dungan, H., & Dungan, J. (n.d.). You Can Make the Pathway Bright. *LDS Hymns*, p. 228.

Ecological Agricultural Projects. (1991). *Nutritional Characteristics of Breads.* Retrieved from Ecological Agricultural Projects: http://eap.mcgill.ca/publications/EAP35.htm

Eyring, H. B. (2005, July). A Discussion on Scripture Study. *Ensign.*

Eyring, H. B. (2005, November). Spiritual Preparedness: Start Early and Be Steady. *Ensign.*

Fallon, S., & Enig, M. G. (1999). *Nourishing Traditions.* New Trends.

Fee, E. (2011). *One Hundred Years Young the Natural Way.* Mississauga, Ont, Canada: Trafford Publishing.

Food Marketing Institute. (2011). *Supermarket Facts.* Retrieved from Food Marketing Institute: http://www.fmi.org/facts_figs/?fuseaction=superfact

For the Strength of Youth. (2011). Salt Lake City, UT: Church of Jesus Christ of Latter-Day Saints.

Fuhrman M.D., J. (2003). *Eat to Live.* New York: Little, Brown and Company.

Grant, H. J. (1937). Conference Report. (p. 15). Church of Jesus Christ of Latter-day Saints.

Handbook 2: Administering the Church. (2010). Salt Lake City, UT: The Church of Jesus Christ of Latter-Day Saints.

Hallstrom, D. L. (2010, May). Turn to the Lord. *Ensign.*

Hinckley, G. B. (1990, November). Mormon Should Mean "More Good". *Ensign.*

Holland, J. R. (2007, May). The Tongue of Angels. *Ensign.*

Holland, J. R. (2012, May). The Laborers in the Vineyard. *Ensign.*

Hunter, H. W. (1994, May). What Manner of Men Ought Ye to Be? *Ensign.*

Insel, P., Ross, D., McMahon, K., & Bernstein, M. (2011).

Nutrition. Sudbury, MA: Jones & Bartlett Learning.

Kang, J. (2008). *Bioenergetics Primer for Exercise Science*. Human Kinetics.

Kimball, S. W. (1974, January). The Rewards, the Blessings, the Promises. *Ensign*, p. 14.

Lawler, C. (2008, December). *Bread Dread - Are You Really Gluten Intolerant?* Retrieved from Nourished Magazine: http://nourishedmagazine.com.au/blog/articles/bread-dread-are-you-really-gluten-intolerant

Live Strong. (2012). *Number of Grams of Protein Intake*. Retrieved from Live Strong: http://www.livestrong.com/article/399188-the-average-grams-of-protein-intake-in-the-average-daily-diet/

Maxwell, N. A. (1993, May). Behold, the Enemy Is Combined. *Ensign*, p. 76.

Mayo Clinic. (2012). *Dietary Fats*. Retrieved from mayoclinic.com: http://www.mayoclinic.com/health/fat/NU00262

Mayo Clinic. (2012). *Nutrition and Healthy Eating*. Retrieved from http://www.mayoclinic.com/health/fiber/NU00033

McDougall M.D., J. A. (2007, Nov). *Vitamin B12 Deficiency*. Retrieved from drmcdougall.com: http://drmcdougall.com/misc/2007nl/nov/b12.htm

McDougall M.D., J. A. (2012). *High Protein Diet*. Retrieved from drmcdougall.com: http://www.drmcdougall.com/res_high_protein_diets.html

McDougall M.D., J. A. (2012, Feb). *Excerpt from the Starch Solution*. Retrieved from drmcdougall.com: http://www.drmcdougall.com/misc/2012nl/feb/120200.pdf

Merrill, J. F. (1978, April). Eat Flesh Sparingly. *Conference Report*, 70-75.

Monson, T. S. (2008, October). Standards of Strength. *New Era*.

Morter D. C., M. T. (1987). *Correlative Urinalysis: The Body Knows Best*. Rogers, Arkansas: B.E.S.T. Research, Inc.

Morter D.C., M. T. (1995). *Dynamic Health*. B.E.S.T. Research, Inc.

Morter D.C., M. T. (1996). *An Apple a Day*. Rogers, Arkansas:

B.E.S.T. Research Inc.

Must, A. J. (1999). The Disease Burden Associated with Overweight and Obesity. *JAMA, 282*(16), pp. 1523-29.

Nano SRT. (2012). *Nano SRT*. Retrieved from http://www.nanosrt.com/

National Institutes of Health. (2012). *Medline Plus - Minerals*. Retrieved from http://www.nlm.nih.gov/medlineplus/minerals.html

Nelson, R. M. (1995, November). Perfection Pending. *Ensign*.

Nutrition Data. (2012). *Self Nutrition Data*. Retrieved from http://nutritiondata.self.com/

Oaks, D. H. (1999, August). Judge Not and Judging. *Ensign*, p. 7.

Oaks, D. H. (2010, May). Healing the Sick. *Ensign*, 47.

Ornish M.D, D. (1995). *Dr. Dean Ornish's Program for Reversing Heart Disease*. Random House.

Packer, B. K. (1996, May). The Word of Wisdom: The Principle and the Promises. *Ensign*, p. 17.

Packer, B. K. (2001, May). The Touch of the Master's Hand. *Ensign*.

Packer, B. K. (2003, Feb 2). *The Instrument of Your Mind and the Foundation of Your Character*. Retrieved from speeches.byu.edu: http://speeches.byu.edu/reader/reader.php?id=478

Packer, B. K. (2005, April). Brilliant Morning of Forgiveness. *New Era*.

Perry, L. T. (2008, November). Let Him do it with Simplicity. *Ensign*.

Philpott, T. (2011, April 6). *Grist*. Retrieved from The American Diet: http://grist.org/industrial-agriculture/2011-04-05-american-diet-one-chart-lots-of-fats-sugars/

Poelman, R. E. (1993, November). Divine Forgiveness. *Ensign*.

Poulter, S. (2010, Mar 5). *Why Frozen Vegetables are Fresher than Fresh*. Retrieved Feb 2012, from Daily Mail: http://www.dailymail.co.uk/health/article-1255606/Why-frozen-vegetables-fresher-fresh.html

Random House, Inc. (2012). *Prudent*. Retrieved from Dictionary.com: http://dictionary.reference.com/browse/prudent

Refined Sugar History. (2011). Retrieved from wholevegan.com: http://www.wholevegan.com/refined_sugar_history.html

Richards, L. (1950). *A Marvelous Work and a Wonder.* P.O. Box 30178, Salt Lake City, Utah 84130: Deseret Book Company.

Roberts, B. H. (1904). *History of the Church of Jesus Christ of Latter-Day Saints, Part 1, Vol 2.* Salt Lake City: The Church of Jesus Christ of Latter-Day Saints.

Schmidt, M. A. (2004). *Childhood Ear Infections.* North Atlantic Books.

Scott, R. G. (1982, August 10). To the Lonely and Misunderstood. *BYU Devotionals.* Retrieved from http://speeches.byu.edu/?act=viewitem&id=471

Scott, R. G. (1995, November). Trust in the Lord. *Ensign.*

Scott, R. G. (2010, March). Finding Forgiveness. *New Era.*

Scott, R. G. (2011, November). The Power of Scripture. *Ensign.*

Scott, R. G. (2012, May). How to Obtain Revelation and Inspiration for Your Personal Life. *Ensign.*

Sherman Ph.D., H. C. (1914). *Food Products.* New York: MacMillan.

Sherman, D. M. (2002). *Tending Animals in the Global Village.* John Wiley & Sons.

Smith, A. F. (2007). *The Oxford companion to American food and drink.* Oxford University Press.

Smith, J. F. (1912, December). The Mexican Trouble. *Improvement Era.*

Smith, J. F. (1947). *Church History and Modern Revelation* (Vol. 2). Salt Lake City, UT: Deseret Book Company.

Smith, J. F. (1949). *Church History and Modern Revelation* (Vol. 1). Salt Lake City, UT: Deseret News Press.

Smith, J. F. (1957). *Answers to Gospel Questions, Vol.1.* P.O. Box 30178, Salt Lake City, UT 84130: Deseret Book Company.

Stapley, D. L. (1961, Oct). Be Ware of Conspiring Men. *Conference Report*, 21-24.

Stewart, R. M. (1950). A Normal Day in the Life of George Albert Smith. *Improvement Era.*

Talmage, J. E. (1915). *Jesus the Christ.* Salt Lake City: Deseret Book.

Tanner, N. E. (1972, Feb). Walking in Obedience to the Commandments. *Ensign*, p. 2.

The American Heritage® Stedman's Medical Dictionary. (2012). Houghton Mifflin Company.

The Cancer Project. (2012). *Diet and Cancer Research.* Retrieved from The Cancer Project: http://www.cancerproject.org/diet_cancer/type/breast/survival.php

The Church of Jesus Christ of Latter-day Saints. (2011). *For the Strength of Youth.* The Church of Jesus Christ of Latter-day Saints.

The Thermic Effect of Food. (2012). Retrieved Feb 28, 2012, from Calories per Hour: http://www.caloriesperhour.com/tutorial_thermic.php

Tsimihodimos, V., Kakaidi, V., & Elisaf, M. (2009, June). *Cola-induced hypokalaemia: pathophysiological mechanisms and clinical implications.* Retrieved from PubMed: http://www.ncbi.nlm.nih.gov/pubmed/19490200

Tuttle, A. T. (1978, Jan 31). *BYU Devotional - Principles With a Promise.* Retrieved from speeches.byu.edu: http://speeches.byu.edu/?act=viewitem&id=1063

Uchtdorf, D. F. (2009, January). Becoming Like Jesus Christ. *Liahona.*

Uchtdorf, D. F. (2011, November). You Matter to Him. *Ensign.*

Uchtdorf, D. F. (2012, May). The Merciful Obtain Mercy. *Ensign.*

USDA. (2005). *The U.S. Grain Consumption Landscape.* Retrieved from USDA: http://www.ers.usda.gov/publications/err50/err50.pdf

USDA. (2005). *US Food Consumption.* Retrieved from Amber Wave: http://www.ers.usda.gov/AmberWaves/November05/findings/usfoodconsumption.htm

USDA. (2012). *How Much Food From the Dairy Group is Needed Daily.* Retrieved from choosemyplate.gov: http://www.choosemyplate.gov/food-groups/dairy-amount.html

Vitamin C History. (2012). Retrieved from Beta Force: http://www.beta-glucan-info.com/vitaminchistory.htm

Wangen, S. (2012). *Milk Allergies and Lactose Intolerance.* Retrieved from Center for Food Allergies: http://centerforfoodallergies.com/milk_allergies.htm#part 2

Whole Grains Council. (2012). *Sprouted Whole Grains.* Retrieved from Whole Grains Council: http://www.wholegrainscouncil.org/whole-grains-101/sprouted-whole-grains

Widstoe, J. A. (1926). Conference Report. Church of Jesus Christ of Latter-day Saints.

Widstoe, J. A. (1937). *Word of Wisdom: A Modern Interpretation.* Salt Lake City, UT.

Widstoe, J. A. (1945). The Staff of Life. *Improvement Era.*

Widstoe, J. A. (1951). *Evidences and Reconcilations* (Vol. 3). Bookcraft.

Wikipedia. (2012). *Amino Acids.* Retrieved from http://en.wikipedia.org/wiki/Amino_acid

Wikipedia. (2012). *Essential Fatty Acids.* Retrieved from http://en.wikipedia.org/wiki/Essential_fatty_acid

Wikipedia. (2012). *Vitamin B12.* Retrieved Mar 2 2012, from Wikipedia: http://en.wikipedia.org/wiki/Vitamin_b12

Wilde, B. R. (2006). *The Liahona Principle.* Springville, UT: Cedar Fort, Inc.

Wilde, B. R. (2011). *The Safe Box of Health.* Wilde Natural Health Publishing.

Winter M.S., R. (2004). *A Consumer's Dictionary of Food Additives.* New York: Three Rivers Press.

Wirthlin, J. B. (2004, April). Earthly Debts, Heavenly Debts. *Ensign.*

Wolinsky, I., & Driskell, J. A. (2008). *Sports nutrition: Energy Metabolism and Exercise.* CRC Press.

Young, B. (1869). *Journal of Discourses* (Vol. 12). Deseret Book.

Young, B. (1877). *Journal of Discourses.* Salt Lake City: Church of Jesus Christ of Latter-day Saints.

About the Author

Bradley R. Wilde was born and raised in Welling, Alberta, Canada, received his doctor of chiropractic degree from Logan Chiropractic College in St. Louis, Missouri and has spent his career as a health care professional in Worland, Wyoming. For more than 30 years he has been passionate about natural health care and wellness, and has taught numerous classes, workshops and seminars on natural healing.

Dr. Wilde's approach to health is based on the principles expounded in this book. He believes that the body knows how to heal itself and that the secret to healing is identifying and treating the cause of the symptom or disease, whether the cause is of a physical, nutritional or emotional nature.

Brother Wilde has served in numerous callings in the Church, including stake president, mission president's councilor, and bishop, all of which significantly increased his understanding of how sin and stress play a role in a person's health.

Dr. Wilde is the author of *The Safe Box of Health – 3 Steps to Heal Yourself,* a book about the steps you must take to heal yourself and be well. He is also the author of *The Liahona Principle,* a book about finding personal direction and understanding in the scriptures, and *It Pays to Understand the Book of Mormon,* a children's workbook.

He and his wife Debi reside in Worland, Wyoming where Dr. Wilde treats and coaches his patients to optimal health. They are the parents of seven wonderful children and seven beautiful grandchildren.

Brad would love to hear how the principles of the Word of Wisdom have blessed your life. You may contact him and find his other books through his website www.drwilde.com.

Made in the USA
Charleston, SC
15 November 2012